"My Name is Justice -
Justice in the Round."

Harold Michael Harvey
April 12, 2015
36/100

JUSTICE in the ROUND

Essays on the American Jury System

Harold Michael Harvey

Copyright © 2015 by Harold Michael Harvey

All rights reserved. No part of this book may be reproduced, stored, or transmitted by any means-whether auditory, graphic, mechanical, electronic or by any means now know or hereafter invented-without written permission of the author, except in the case of brief excerpts used in critical articles and reviews.

ISBN: 9780692400555
PUBLISHED BY: CASCADE PUBLISHING HOUSE
Atlanta, Georgia
Haroldmichaelharvey.com

Manufactured in the United States of America

"Democracy is the only ideology consistent with freedom that codifies those freedoms and the denial of those freedoms with equal zeal to those subjected to its codified rules."

Peter Popham – "The Lady and the Peacock: The Life of Aung San Suukyi of Burma"

Dedication

This book is dedicated to Emmett, Troy, Trayvon, Jordan, Kendrick, Michael, Eric, Africa and unknown others. Their ability to grow into manhood cut short by one form of legal lynching or another.

"The legal system can force open doors and sometimes even knock down walls. But it cannot build bridges. That job belongs to you and me."

*Justice Thurgood Marshall
United States Supreme Court*

Table of Contents

Acknowledgments

Opening Statement   7

"They Always Get Away"   15

Zimmerman not Guilty   57

Simmering with Zimmerman:
James Baldwin's 'The Fire Next Time' Revisited   62

Obama's Soul on Ice:
A Week Later and I'm Still Numb   70

Whites Are Dodging Obama's Call for an Honest Discussion on Race   76

The killings of Trayvon Martin and Jordan Davis:
More Creepy White Crap   83

How Can a Black Juror not see Race in the Loud-Music Trial?   89

The Jury System Was Designed for Europeans to Judge Europeans   95

How Do White Men get Away with Killing Black Teenagers?   100

Speaking Truth in the Jury Room   106

On the Evil in the Abyss   112

Closing Argument   120

"Appreciation is a wonderful thing. It makes what is excellent in others belong to us as well."

Voltaire

ACKNOWLEDGMENT

I owe the inspiration for this book on the relevancy of the jury system in American jurisprudence in the brave new world of the 21st century to Lesley Joy Allen, a doctoral history student at Georgia State University who suggested I put my thoughts on the jury system in book form.

I am indebted to Allvoices, Inc. where several essays on this subject were first published. I owe a special thanks to the editorial guidance of Darren Richardson, better known as "Punditty" at Allvoices, for his editorial assistance on the commentaries published at Allvoices.com. He is a stickler for details. He checks every fact and every source to ensure that quotes are exact and that names are spelled correctly. The words on this page are not adequate to express his contribution to this book.

Patricia Marsh, the consummate school teacher, lent her teacher's eye to the text and provided valuable input to the final manuscript.

Also, Cherrie Welch finely tuned eye surveyed several of the essays that were originally published in Allvoices and made several suggestions on the cover design.

Additionally, Willis Perry was helpful in suggesting the theme for the cover design.

Every writer needs a good reader or two. For me those persons are Terry Wiggins and Rutha De Jesus. Thanks for taking first crack at my rough prose and giving me the benefit of your thoughts.

Coley Harvey, a sports writer at ESPN, who continues to pay dividends for the sacrifice we made in sending him to the Medill School of Journalism at Northwestern, made sure that the *Associated Press Stylebook* and *The Chicago Manual of Style* were properly represented throughout these pages.

Of course, where would I be without my senior editor of 35 years?

Cyn Harvey is a wordsmith's wordsmith. I can count on her to always search for the perfect word to replace the perfect word I had selected to paint a vivid picture for my readers. The interaction with her to pull out of me, a clearer word with even more precise meaning is one of the simple pleasures that I enjoy in life.

We all, dear readers, owe a great debt of gratitude to my mother, Elaine Harvey, who nurtured my writing skills in the early days, by finding money on a tight budget to enroll me in a correspondence writing course at the Palmer Institute, and told me like the little train that said, "I think I can, I think I can, I think can," that, indeed I can.

"How came my children to be what they are? From what ancestry did they get this strain? How far removed was the poison that destroyed their lives? Was I the bearer of the seed that brings them to death?"

– *Clarence Darrow, Chicago, 1924*

"We who desire justice, must of necessity, end the real causes of injustice, therefore, Semper Novi Quid ex Injustice!"

Harold Michael Harvey

FOREWORD

This book does not offer any proposals for the reform of the jury system that was designed by the framers of the constitution more than 225 years ago.

Many of my friends, who learned of my efforts to address the jury system in light of the George Zimmerman and Michael Dunn acquittals for killing, within eight months of each other, two teenage African American boys in Florida, wrote to suggest ways the system could be improved.

Some people suggested that the jury system should be abolished in its entirety as the system is simply unjust. Given that our present system was devised to correct a problem the framers were intimately familiar with from the English system. It was a system where previously a person could be held indefinitely, without charges, without benefit of counsel, or the benefit of having the Crown to provide proof of guilt. What we have today is a far better way to regulate the conduct of those subjected to the rules of a democratic society.

Others saw the problem in the system of preemptory challenges and suggested that reducing the number of challenges the state and defense could make to remove prospective jurors would solve the problem. As a very active trial lawyer in the last decade of the 20th century, I always wished I had just one more jury strike. There seemed to be one juror that sneaked under the radar because all of my preemptory challenges had been used on the more obviously biased jurors.

Many saw the jury system as being easily manipulated by the attorneys and called for more ethical decisions by attorneys when picking a jury. In defense of trial lawyers, they are charged with selecting the best jurors who will view the evidence in the most favorable light to their client.

As long as the lawyers follow the criminal procedure in their jurisdiction for selecting jurors, they cannot be faulted for opting for the juror who is most likely to be fair to their client, as opposed to one who will not be guided by a sense of fairness.

A number of people thought the lawyers tried to pick the least intelligent members of the venire, a panel of prospective jurors, from which, twelve of the fairest minds of the community are selected to decide issues of guilt or innocence.

Lawyers can only work with the individuals that the courts present to them at the commencement of the trial. The jury pools are now drawn from the various voter registration lists in the jurisdictions where the trials are held. There may be some validity to this concern.

Trial lawyers, from my continuing legal education experience, are trained to avoid other lawyers, medical doctors, tax accountants, psychologists, in short, anyone who can logically add one plus two, and come up with three.

There were some who thought that the number of jurors should be limited. A minority of state jurisdictions allow a six-person jury to decide criminal matters, in cases where the criminally accused has waived his right to the federal constitutional right to a jury of twelve.

Others suggested that a panel of professional jurors trained in the law would remedy the situation. We've witnessed what a mess such a system of jurors trained in the law has done in the Italian murder trial of Amanda Knox. Is she guilty or not guilty? A legally trained jury, after several years and multiple trials, as of the publication of these essays, is still out.

I find no fault in these suggestions; however, modification of the jury system is not the scope of my epistles on this topic. I did not set out to fix what some perceive as a broken system.

There are others who are smarter than I and thus better equipped to address the esoteric rudiments of putting a band aid on a systemic problem that dates back to colonial America.

My mission was to understand the philosophical, psychological, and sociological attribution which every prospective juror brings to the courthouse when they receive a summons to appear on the threat of being arrested if they do not show up.

When I worked as a trial lawyer, I recognized that being a prospective juror is fraught with embarrassment. It is not an easy thing to sit in a big courtroom, filled with strangers, and as the legal jargon goes, publish intimate details about your work, home, family and religious life, or lack thereof, or any of those things which society portends are the characteristics of a wholesome life.

Every day hundreds of ordinary American citizens do it. It is the biases and prejudices that come with the jurors, which filter out in this sifting process. Prospects, then, are either stricken from the venire or end up on the jury deciding the fate of some member of the community.

These biases and prejudices of prospective jurors may side with the biases and prejudices of the accused or they may be contrary to the accuser's way of life. It is the job of the skilled trial lawyer to ferret out those biases and prejudices before the first item of evidence is offered for the jury's consideration.

One salient fact shapes my frame of reference in these essays: All jurors bring to the jury room their genetics and their sundry environments. By virtue of this fact, we are all subconsciously race-conscious. No one can divorce themselves from their genetic make-up, but we can, if we choose, overcome the environmental conditions that enable us to be fair to people with different genetics and social standing.

Let's get it out in the open from the starting line, or in the vernacular of my youth, "from the git go."

Race, as I see it, is the biggest problem in getting fair jury deliberations in American courtrooms today. Race, that unspoken problem dating back to the dawn of Colonial American civilization rules the jury box every time the dichotomy of race is a factor in criminal prosecutions.

Usually, the hue and cry following a perceived unjust jury verdict tends to be the loudest in cases where the issues involved contestants from different racial or cultural backgrounds. This is especially true in cases where the majority of the jury is composed of persons from the racial or cultural background of the "prevailing" party.

Before anyone throws the reverse race card, do not be so quick to misunderstand me. Also know this; my skin has been sufficiently toughened over the years to withstand the missiles of misguided closet racists.

Moreover, this list includes the unsuspecting racial biases inherently present by virtue of the complexities of life we all are required to navigate each day.

Do not be offended if I have included you in the universal set of "closet racists," as everyone, including this writer, starts out in this universal set. Only time tells whether any of us will ever escape this status. Our ranks are legion and are only closeted because we are not aware that we harbor racial feelings.

ESSAY 1

Opening Statement

Before throwing down the race card, get through the essay where the prospective juror in one of my trials asked a courthouse deputy: "What do you think about that Nigger lawyer from Atlanta?"

Additionally, as you read these essays, if the proverbial racist shoes do not fit, then do not attempt to wear them. If they fit your neighbors, why not have a frank and honest discussion with them. After all, we are trying to get to a better place.

Now that the issue of race is out front and center, we begin these essays on the American jury system with one titled *"They always get away."*

For the purposes of this essay we are paraphrasing what George Zimmerman told the 911 dispatch operator when the dispatcher told him not to follow Trayvon Martin. Zimmerman actually said: "Those a-- holes always get away."

He was referring to the African American men who lived in the ghetto outside the gates of his middle-class townhouse community.

Because these situations (the wholesale murder of black teenagers) do not happen in a vacuum, *"They always get away"* is a rambling history from the reconstruction era of American history through today's headlines.

This history lesson is told through the eyes of the writer and those of a college classmate, Cheryl Lattimore. It is a personal journey through the events that shaped the last half of the 20th century. Cheryl, in a Facebook communiqué, challenged me to look beyond the Zimmerman jury verdict for possible systemic relief. She pushed and prodded me as only an old friend can do, expecting that if anyone could pin down the problems confronting justice in America her old political science classmate could do it.

Her challenge reminded me of a knock on my front door early one morning in the late winter of 2010. My neighbor, Rev. Dr. C. T. Vivian, who was destined to become a 2013 recipient of the Presidential Medal of Freedom, had a dream as he slept during the night and had walked down to my house to share it with me. He was concerned with the incarceration rate of African American young men.

He recalled my interest in the 1990s in encouraging African American athletes to pursue a career in baseball. Vivian, a rangy first baseman in his youth, wanted me to help establish a baseball academy that would teach baseball skills to black youngsters to prepare them for a career in major league baseball. This would provide these youngsters who felt trapped in poverty with a skill set that could engage their talents at a hefty annual salary for twenty years or more. This would, he thought, decrease the number of black teenage men from committing criminal acts, some of which were violent acts, to sustain themselves and their families.

For several hours, we talked about how to incorporate a baseball academy into the C. T. Vivian Institute, which he was planning to create. Then I walked him back up the hill to his house. He confided in me that the real problem facing the African American community is the fact that coming out of the period of enslavement, Africans were not compensated for their forced labor. Instead their descendants have been running in place for over one hundred and fifty years attempting to catch up with the descendants of Americans who never knew bondage on these shores.

Vivian asked if I would research the issue of reparations. He said reparations would be a good way to cap off his life. It would, he opined, solve the issue of poverty and racism which lead to so many young African Americans being incarcerated.

No doubt, this is a daunting task. A task which I felt ill prepared to undertake. Besides that reparation, alias, "forty-acres and a mule," had been talked about since 1865, but no administration has had the courage or political will to put up the capital to get it done.

How then, does one say no to Dr. Vivian, a stalwart of Selma, whose verbal joist with Sheriff Jim Clarke inspired marchers to gather courage to cross the Edmund Pettis Bridge on "Bloody Sunday"?

You do not. Instead, you tell him, you will give some thought to it.

I did.

I placed the thought of "reparatory justice" in the back of my mind. There it stayed for several years, until my old friend, Cheryl, prodded me to do something more than anybody else was doing to come up with a solution to the killing of young black men on the streets of America.

The something more is contained in *"They always get away"* and this essay should be read in light of Vivian's quest for intergenerational justice for descendants of enslaved Africans in America.

Toward the end Cheryl gives a new twist to the phrase *"They always get away," tres decimas similae in justitia,* which perhaps, may point to a possible solution.

"Zimmerman not Guilty" announces the cold, harsh reality of what happens when a "white-on-black" killing occurs in a town with a tiny minority of black citizens. It was written the night the Zimmerman opinion came back, July 13, 2013.

As is my journalistic practice, I had written the basic story following closing arguments, and was waiting for the jury's verdict to come in so I could fill in the details of the verdict. I have to admit, I was stunned that Zimmerman got away with what many perceive was a blatant act of murder.

Following the Zimmerman jury verdict, the nation (or at least the black and progressive portion of it) was simmering and on the brink of explosion. Fearing an eruption of violence in urban America, Rev. Al Sharpton, called for multiple demonstrations throughout the country.

Sharpton, a year earlier, aroused the nation and forced the Governor of Florida to appoint a Special State Attorney to handle this case.

"Simmering with Zimmerman: James Baldwin's The Fire Next Time revisited" grew out of the aftermath of the national frustration over the Zimmerman jury's verdict.

Had Sharpton called a mass rally in Sanford, Florida following the Zimmerman verdict, like he had done prior to Zimmerman's arrest, a powder keg would likely have produced the fire this time.

"Obama's Soul on Ice: A week later and I'm still numb," explores how the system of things, therefore, the status quo, has placed a very talented and very black President on ice which numbs the fibers of my nervous system as well. It was written, obviously, a week after the Zimmerman verdict was published to the nation.

"Whites are dodging Obama's Call for an Honest Discussion on Race," points out the fact that a dialogue on race is a two-way street. The real discussion on race is one that must occur

among white people where they face-up to the reality of white privilege and come to some decision that they are willing to forego the perks of skin color for the common good of all.

"*The killing of Trayvon Martin and Jordan Davis: More creepy white mess,*" grew out of Trayvon Martin's description to Rachel Jeantel of the man who was stalking him moments before his death. We have paraphrased his actual words, which were: "Creepy-ass white cracker."

"*How can a black juror not see race in the loud-music trial?*" This piece explores the psychology of twenty-something-year-old African Americans who do not have a personal civil rights or Jim Crow past. Other ethnic Americans can learn from this essay as well. Just substitute the "twenty-something-year-old African Americans" with your limited knowledge of the African American experience from colonial America through the age of Obama.

"*The jury system was designed for Europeans to judge Europeans,*" gets to the heart of the problem with the administration of justice by way of a peer-jury system.

"*How do white men get away with killing black teenagers?*" This section deals with the practical application of striking a jury. After reading this essay, if you are still inclined to play the race card, now would be the time to do it.

"*Speaking truth in the jury room,*" discusses the focus of the Zimmerman and Dunn jurors. We conclude that they were doing the judge's job and not that of the jury. In our system of Jurisprudence, the judge is judge of the law and the jury is the judge of the facts. Both of these juries (the Zimmerman and Dunn juries) got their mission, in the lexicon of today's youth, "twisted."

Our closing argument on the American jury system is *"On the evil in the abyss,"* an account of the legal, state-approved killing of Troy Davis, by the state of Georgia, in the face of a tremendous volume of doubt concerning his guilt.

The Davis segment points out, all too often, what happens under the American jury system, when the accused is black and the victim is white. The weight of the evidence, no matter how light, tends to go against the black defendant.

Dear readers, I hope this little book will inspire you to work for candid and frank discussions about race. I hope that white and other ethnic readers will realize that it is okay for black people to be black people.

Yet just as important as the fact that black people are black; when brought before the court, either as victims, or the accused; they should be afforded every benefit of the doubt that the law allows.

I hope black readers will reach out to their white friends and associates with love and understanding, while their white friends and associates are breaking away from the shackles of privilege that have enslaved them for centuries, like the physical and mental shackles, which have enslaved Africans in America for centuries.

At long last, this solemn volume owes no duty to political correctness. Its fidelity is to the truth as witnessed by the writer. Let us hope, that out of the seemingly unjust verdicts in the Zimmerman and Dunn trials, there comes a new sense of justice for all.

The Cascades -- Atlanta, Georgia

March 15, 2014

Essay 2

"They always get away"

"The only thing that white people have that black people should need or want is power and no one holds power forever."

*James Baldwin,
"The Fire Next Time"*

"Write something," the simple command posted on my Facebook wall said. It was the summer of 2009. I was in a dead zone waiting for the release of my first novel, *"Paper Puzzle,"* from my first publisher, whose name will go unmentioned as our relationship soured after a year and I was forced to move into the self-publishing industry where I learned the pains and joys of the publishing trade on my own and at my own expense.

At any rate, I was in a period where time seemingly stood still and I didn't quite know what to do with myself. My novel had been put to bed, as we say in the industry.

There wasn't much to do until the release date. I wasn't sure how my work would be received, how I would be accepted on the book tour circuit, or if I would even make any money from this endeavor.

I have those same pains of uncertainty upon the pending release of these essays. A writer never knows when he or she has hit the ball out of the park. Only time and an attentive audience of readers will determine the fate of the witness we bear.

This command to "write something" did not come from the Facebook prompt to begin a discussion with my social media friends; it came from Cheryl Lattimore, a flesh and blood friend, whom I have known since 1970, as opposed to a cyber optic bot, which we all tend to spend more time talking with in this technological age; an age, which causes us to willingly give up our privacy and share intimate details of our lives with complete strangers we may never see face-to-face.

So I began this rambling essay with the working title "Write Something", and as the spirit has touched me over the course of the last four years, I have added to it, finally settling on the title, "They Always Get Away."

A lot has happened in four years. The first African American elected President of the United States was sworn into office. Immediately, it became an act of racism for anyone to disclose they had voted for him. Those bold enough to do so were met with the refrain, "You only voted for him because he was black," the politics of the reverse race card was now being played by many white Americans. None of whom bothered to think that in the age before Obama, black voters voted in mass for white presidential contenders simply because only white men were ever nominated for the office. Black people have never had a problem with voting for white candidates. In fact, more black people have voted for white candidates than there are white people who have voted for a black candidate.

Almost as soon as President Barack Obama commenced his service, he was rejected, vilified and blocked at every turn to carry out the duties of his office, by a group, which cannot in all honesty be described, as the loyal opposition.

CHANGE THE NAME
AND CHANGE THE CULTURE

Cheryl and I met in a political science class at Tuskegee Institute; that pragmatic institution of a programmatic solution anointed to bring the American Negro up out of several centuries of enslavement and into the 19th Century, by the former enslaved, with help from those who decried their enslavement.

The Institute, as it was called back then, was founded in 1881, two days after President James A. Garfield was shot (July 2, 1881) by Charles Giuteau. On July 4, 1881, Booker T. Washington arrived at the train depot at Chehaw, Alabama to commence the first classroom instruction and his work of a lifetime.

Earlier in the year, on February 12, 1881 the Alabama Legislature had appropriated the sum of $2,000 annually for the establishment of a "normal school" at Tuskegee for the education of teachers. "Normal schools" today are known as teacher's colleges.

The tuition would be free in exchange for the student's pledge to teach for two years in the black school houses of Alabama. Tuskegee was not a land-grant college as the initial land for the school was donated by Lewis Adams, formerly enslaved by the landed gentry in East Alabama. Later, Washington raised money to buy an abandoned plantation (500,000 acres), on the site where the university stands today.

Adams, a well-established shopkeeper in the town of Tuskegee, donated the land for the school after he parlayed a political deal that swung the 1880 Macon County, Alabama, black vote away from the Republican Party to re-elect two vulnerable white Democratic state legislators.

Garfield died of his wounds two months after he was shot. Washington was two months into his experiment at Tuskegee, which would see him lobby every American president from Chester Arthur to Woodrow Wilson.

In 1881, for the second time in the nation's history, three men served as President within the same year. Rutherford B. Hayes, who pulled the federal troops out of the South and opened the door to a reign of terror by southern white men determined to block the full re-construction of black people into the rich fabric of American life, served out his one and only term. [1]

Garfield, Hayes' successor and friend died in September and was replaced by his Vice President, Chester Arthur. It was on the backdrop of the ending of the Hayes presidency, a presidency, which unreconstructed the South where the Tuskegee experiment began.

By the early 1900s Washington had established schools using the Tuskegee model in West Africa, in what is present day Ghana. Like Tuskegee, those schools continue operating on the principals taught by Washington.

---

[1] Back in the 19th century, the presidential term was four years, but from April to March of the fourth year, instead of beginning on January 20th of the fourth year and ending on January 20th of the fourth year.

It is a misnomer of history to recognize Washington as the "Great Founder" of the Tuskegee legacy. He was not. The ideal that became Tuskegee was conceived by Adams, the Negro shopkeeper on the town square. He believed that by working with the hands, Negroes could secure the financial means to take care of their families and gain the trust and respect of the whites to whom they would provide these services for pay.

Thus, Tuskegee was the genius of Adams, who parlayed his political muscle for a line item in Alabama's educational budget. Before the Tuskegee experiment, when schools were established for the colored freedmen, white men were called upon to preside over those black colleges. One exception was the Atlanta Baptist Female Seminary, founded in 1881, later named Spelman College, which was headed by a white woman, Sophia Packard.

Adams envisioned a strong Negro community in America that was self-sufficient; a mirror image of the best in white America. His foresight insisted upon selecting a Negro to head up the school.

For the next 34 years, Washington literally worked himself to death to inculcate Adam's vision into descendants of former enslaved Africans in the United States of America.

In the beginning, the days following the suppression of the southern states' revolt, were plagued with fear and mistrust between white people and their newly acquired fellow Americans.

The nation was also plagued by a dire need for blacks to acquire the skills and education to live in a "so-called" civilized society. Those blacks had, for the most part, been hewers of wood and clogs in someone else's commercial profit center while being stripped of all sense of human dignity and socialization.

It was incumbent upon those, like Adams and Washington, who had lived in the big house with their masters and had seen the ways of white men, to bring their brothers and sisters out of the fields of centuries of dis-socialization and inhumane treatment by teaching them the ways and mores of their new country.

Washington's task was compounded by Hayes' acquiescence to the demands of Southern gentlemen who wanted to roll-back the political clock to pre-Reconstruction and pre-Civil War days. Their demands asked Hayes to cancel the gains made by these new citizens in the political affairs on the state and federal level with passage of the 13th amendment. Also, they called for the birth of a second-tier of citizenship to be established for those given the privilege of American citizenship pursuant to the 13th amendment.

Ralph Ellison, in his novel "Invisible Man," depicts the climate of the days immediately following the southern revolt, which thrust Washington into action:

"And then his great struggle beginning.

Picture it, my young friends: The clouds of darkness all over the land, black folk and white folk full of fear and hate, wanting to go forward, but each fearful of the other. A whole region is caught in a terrible tension. Everyone is perplexed with the question of what must be done to dissolve this fear and hatred that crouched over the land like a demon waiting to spring..., his great humility and his undimming vision, the fruits of which you enjoy today; concrete, made flesh, his dream, conceived in the starkness and darkness of slavery, fulfilled now even in the air you breathe, in the sweet harmonies of your blended voices, in the knowledge which each of you -- daughters and granddaughters, sons and grandsons, of slaves -- all of you partaking of it in bright and well-equipped classrooms...And your parents followed this remarkable man across the black sea of prejudice, safely out of the land of ignorance, through the storms of fear and anger, shouting, LET MY PEOPLE GO! When it was necessary, whispering it during those times when whispering was wisest. And he was heard."[2]

    In 1915, Washington was silenced by death. He died of a heart attack after traveling all night by train from New York to his beloved Tuskegee. He had been sickened while in New York for several weeks. His wife, Margaret Murray Washington, angered at the doctor for releasing private information about his medical condition, withdrew him from a New York hospital and placed him on a train bound for Tuskegee that "...

---

[2] Invisible Man, Ralph Ellison, Second Vintage International Edition, March 1995, Random House, Inc., pp 119-120

Long striving mother of diligent sons and daughters whose strength is their pride...,"[3] where the Angel, who comes for the "full fruit for thy striving time longer to strive sweet love and labor's reward,"[4] could easily find him, in death.

As late as 1928, Tuskegee Institute was still advocating for reparations for descendants of enslaved Africans.

Washington's successor, Robert Moton, cut a deal with Herbert Hoover to swing support away from the incumbent President, Calvin Coolidge, in exchange for Hoover's pledge to establish farms from land lost in bankruptcy court by white farmers.

Hoover failed to keep his promise after winning the election, so Moton swung his support in 1932 to the Democrat, Franklin Delano Roosevelt, thus beginning the slow migration of black voters away from the Republican fold. Instead of offering descendants of enslaved Africans reparations, Roosevelt offered them a "New Deal" that included social security and public work programs.

The Institute was renamed Tuskegee University at the suggestion of President George Herbert Walker Bush in the mid-1980s. The name change all came about when Bush took the school's fifth President, Dr. Benjamin Payton, on a state visit to Africa.

Bush queried Payton on the meaning of

---

[3] The Tuskegee Song, "The Pride of the Swift Growing South," by Paul Lawrence Dunbar
[4] Ibid

Institute. Payton did not have a good response, with respect to, the ideals Tuskegee Institute institutionalized in the last quarter of the 20th century.

The nation's President told Payton, the Institute's President, that no one in Africa knew anything about Tuskegee and that it was too difficult to explain it to them. Thus, it would be better if Tuskegee was listed as a college or university.

Bush was unaware that the model for Tuskegee Institute had been replicated in Ghana by Washington at the turn of the 20th century, and that Africans were very familiar with Tuskegee Institute and its model of self-sufficiency for Africans on "The Continent" and Africans in the Diaspora. The campus in East Alabama had always had a strong contingent of African students matriculating in its classrooms.

Payton fell for it. He pushed a resolution through the Board of Trustees and the name was changed to "Tuskegee University." Payton posited that because of the many schools that existed within the Institute at that time, it was the appropriate thing to do.[5] At the time, I offered a compromise, Tuskegee Institute University, similar to the naming of Texas Tech University. However, this compromise was rejected and was never discussed publicly.

---

[5] For example, the School of Veterinary Medicine, School of Agriculture, School of Engineering, and the School of Architecture have been well respected for many years.

President Bush's argument did not take into consideration that the historically white Massachusetts Institute of Technology in Boston or the Georgia Institute of Technology in Atlanta were revered the world over and no one bothered to question their academic acumen.

Has either of them ever been called upon to explain their existence, for instance, their reason for being?

Have these schools ever been called upon to explain what they do?

It was, in fact, the success of Tuskegee Institute which led the Georgia legislature to establish the Georgia School of Technology in 1885.[6]

White men in the south could not get jobs in the skilled building professions because many of the educated people in the industry were being trained at Tuskegee Normal and Industrial Institute.

A careful read of history will reveal that following the success of Tuskegee in industrial education, many of the States established Technical colleges. For example, in 1923, Texas created Texas Tech University.

One might argue, the Lone Star State, was moved by the success of Tuskegee in providing technical education in the southeast and opened

---

[6] Georgia Tech did not formally open its doors until 1888; seven years after Booker T. Washington began to flood the construction industry with black electricians, carpenters, brick and mortar experts, designers, and etcetera.

the door to its citizens in the Texas panhandle to compete in face of this emerging demand for a technically trained workforce.

LOOKING BACK TO LOOK FORWARD

Cheryl and I met August 20, 1970, in old Collins P. Huntington Hall, which, until early one August morning in 1991, when a fire burned the interior of the building, gutting it and leaving the brick façade, housed the School of Arts and Sciences. The building had for 86 years, serviced thousands of eager minds, who for the most part, were descended from men and women who had been shackled, forced into ships, stripped of native garb, language, God and human dignity only to toil, unpaid, in the murky still waters of American democracy.

Huntington Hall was the central meeting place for all Tuskegee students at that time. Everyone had to pass through her doors to take the core courses before concentrating on their major course work.

Now the main meeting for Tuskegee students is the National Bio-Ethics Center, formerly the sight of the John A. Andrews Hospital, where the famed Tuskegee Syphilis Study was conducted, when poor black farmers and military veterans were inoculated with the syphilis germ and not provided with a vaccine to cure it. These men unknowingly passed this disease onto their wives and girlfriends. They were used has human guinea pigs.

To be fair, some of them came into the John A. Andrews Hospital seeking treatment with the disease and were also not given a vaccine. They had no idea their sexual partners should be notified to seek treatment. They all were studied to see what the long term effects of this disease would be on the human body.

Collins P. Huntington, one of the famed "Robber Barons" of the 19th Century was solicited by Booker T. Washington to donate money for a building on campus. Huntington, not interested in being known in history as a mere "Robber Baron," contributed a sum of money for the construction of an academic building.

Ellison, in his factious depiction in "Invisible Man" of a historical, black, elite southern university, which many scholars believes is based upon his experiences as a student at Tuskegee Institute, portrays it thusly:

"You must see this slave, this black Aristotle, moving slowly, with sweet patience, with patience not of mere man, but of God-inspired faith -- see him moving slowly as he surmounts each and every opposition. Rendering, unto Caesar that which was Caesar's yes; but steadfastly seeking for you that bright horizon which you now enjoy."[7]

Between 1904 and 1905, second-generation free black men designed a four-story building at Tuskegee under the watchful eye of the first black architect to graduate from the Massachusetts Institute of Technology, Robert Taylor. This

---

[7] Ibid p. 120

massive structure was built on a steep incline, and like the pyramids of Egypt, without benefit of the cranes, so widely used in today's construction.

They then made bricks using the red clay indigenous to the area and mixed a mortar to hold the bricks in place. One-by-one the bricks were stacked atop each other by black hands until Collins P. Huntington had his shrine and Booker T. Washington finally had sufficient classroom space for his work at Tuskegee.

The political science course where Cheryl Lattimore and I met was taught on the third floor of Huntington Hall by Dr. Elechukwu Nnadibuagh Njaka. Dr. Njaka was not an African American. He was an African, without a slave past.

Njaka was a member of the Igbo tribe found in Nigeria, the nation-state that conspired with European slave traders to kidnap and sell men and women from neighboring west African nation-states into enslavement in the western hemisphere.

Nigeria was the first point of sale of human cargo. Money, beads and trinkets first exchanged hands in Nigeria and amounted to a mere fraction of the money that Europeans made in buying and selling human flesh when this human cargo reached western ports.

Any modern day discussion of reparation cannot leave Nigeria out of the equation. Their economy was built on the backs of Africans from the old Ivory Coast and surrounding typography.

In the late 1960s, Njaka became a General in the Army of the Republic of Biafra. He led a revolt that had sought to overthrow the Nigerian government. When the war could not be won, he and his co-patriots fled the battlefield.

Njaka, unlike the descendants of his students, ran as fast as he could, jumped on an airplane bound for the United States and basked in the comfort of the protection, which the United States gave him from his countrymen. Then he put to use his Doctoral Degree in Political Science.

When I received the command to "write something," I gave Cheryl Lattimore a lame excuse. I feigned that coordinating a book-signing tour was taking up all my time.

It was a true statement of current affairs, but no excuse for a writer not to write.

Cheryl knew from the get-go it was a lame excuse. When you have known someone for so long, they can pierce through the bull.

So, you "write something." If only to tell the world how long you have known a good friend. You hope the world will note that men and women can be friends. You hope the world will not misinterpret and thereby denigrate your relationship with your friend. You hope the world will recognize that lasting friendships are built on mutual respect for the intelligence of each other and not by nocturnal sights and sighs.

We met as brother and sister, two intellects trying to find our way in the world of academia. Cheryl grew up in Jackson, Mississippi.

She was 13 years of age and living in Jackson, on June 12, 1963 when Medgar Evers,

Field Secretary for the Mississippi Chapter of the National Association for the Advancement of Colored People, was gunned down in his driveway.

"He was a nice man. He had an office in my neighborhood. He would greet the neighborhood kids with a smile and an encouraging word," is Cheryl's lasting memory of him.

"I had no idea he was a famous man. To me he was just a nice black man dressed in a suit. We would ride our bicycles up to his office and sometimes he would come out and talk with us," Cheryl recalled.

Evers offended the sensibilities of white Mississippians by traveling around the state with gruesome pictures of the aftermath of Klan torture of black people. He called attention to how whites punished blacks who simply wanted to be free to date, to eat, to vote in peace like other Americans.

Evers' approach drew the attention of the 35th President of the United States of America, John F. Kennedy. On the evening of Evers' murder, mere hours before Evers was killed, Kennedy had taken to the national air waves.

Kennedy announced to the nation that the federal government would aggressively pursue the full integration of the American Negro into American life and development.

From Macon, Georgia, I watched Kennedy's national broadcast on the family's black and white television set. You could feel the joy spread through each room of the house.

But then, before we could go to bed and

dream of a better tomorrow, news came that Medgar Evers had been assassinated in his driveway, after a long day of freedom fighting.

Ironically, Evers had joined the fight after witnessing a mob demand the release of a black man from the hospital where the man had been taken after he fought with a white man. Evers said about that incident:

"It seemed that this (racism) would never change. It was that way for my daddy. It was that way for me. And it looked as though it would be that way for my children. I was so mad I just stood there trembling and tears rolled down my cheeks."[8]

"We both knew he was going to die," Myrlie Evers, his widow, later said, "Medgar did not want to be a martyr. But if he had to die to get us that far, he was willing to do it."[9]

In the 1960s, murder, the motif of the white supremacists, filled the headlines of the nation's newspapers. First, murder struck in Mississippi, then Birmingham, then in Dallas, then in Harlem, then in Memphis and in Los Angeles. The decade of the 1960s began with the promise of Camelot and ended awash in the blood of its most daring progressive thinkers.

The pain of those days was etched in my psyche and Cheryl's as she sat next to me in Huntington Hall, seven years after Evers' assassination. She had money for text books, a pretty smile and a boyfriend from South Carolina

---

[8] "Medgar Evers". www.HistoryLearningSite.co.uk.web
[9] Ibid

to occupy her time.

I seldom smiled and had neither a girlfriend nor money for text books. Thus a compact was struck. I could read course work assignments from her text books, as long as I shared what I had read.

Into this mix came another soon-to-be dear friend, Larry Sankey, from Abbeville, Alabama, just a few miles from Dothan, Henry County, Alabama, which was adjoined to and the home county, Bullock, of the segregationist governor, George Wallace.

Before the age of 10, Sankey saw George Wallace, a rather moderate Democrat lose his first race for political office because his white opponent played the "race card." Wallace vowed never again would he be "Out Niggard" by a political opponent; he never was.

Until a would-be assassin's bullet put him in a wheel chair, Wallace was the Donald Trump of "race cards." Drawing on his religious upbringing, Wallace declared on the steps of the University of Alabama in the face of federal troops: "Segregation today, Segregation tomorrow, (and the refrain that sank my young heart every time I heard it) Segregation forever."

Although, I hoped for a day when segregation would not be the law of the land, the way respectable white people embraced the nuances of segregation, I thought, that it would last forever; like the unspoken thought, that a black man, could ever become president of the country.

Cheryl, Larry and I quickly learned the three of us had birthdays within seven days of each other. So we formed a study group. Between using the text books each of them had and the money I earned during the summer months and Christmas breaks waiting on tables at exclusive resorts, I had sufficient money for tuition. Thus an education from Tuskegee Institute was obtained.

In the spring of 1971, while walking to campus from our downtown residence, Steve Duval, Gerald Harvey and I learned that Wallace was going to kick off his second campaign for president of the United States of America in Ozark, Alabama. Gerald and I were political science majors, we figured there was no better way to get an up close and personal educational experience than to attend Wallace's rally. So, the three of us jumped in the car of a guidance counselor employed by the Institute and headed for Ozark, Alabama.

In 1968, Wallace ran for president on the American Independent Party ticket. He polled 13.5 percent of the total vote. More than 9 million Americans voted for his racial divisive politics. He received 46 electoral votes.[10]

That year, Richard Nixon found redemption, as he narrowly out polled Hubert Humphrey in the popular vote by .7% to become the 37th president.[11]

We arrived in Ozark just before dusk,

---
[10] http://uselectionatlas.org/RESULTS/national.php?year=1968
[11] Ibid

dressed in dungarees and Mexican ponchos, bearded, with afros at the maximum length, and eager for a historic educational experience.

We were in for a surprise.

If we had any notion that our white brothers and sisters had cleared their hearts of racial animosity on the day that President Lyndon Johnson had signed the Civil Rights Act of 1964, it disappeared before we took ten steps towards the entrance of the stadium where Wallace was scheduled to speak.

The crowd had begun to assemble. They were cooking food; listening to country music and eating like people do at a football tailgate party. As the sun began to disappear from the horizon, the crowd grew. There were no other Negroes to be found. We were hungry, but dared not stopped to purchase food from one of the food vendors. The word was passed down the line in our group to keep your hands in your pockets and for God's sake, do not bump into any of the white women. Emmitt Till and others had been strung up and castrated for such as that.

What struck me about this assemblage of campaign supporters was the number of new born babies in their mother's arms wrapped in Wallace for President bumper stickers.

We found seats in the stadium away from the crowd. Wallace's helicopter hovered over the stadium, but did not land. We could not figure out why he had not landed; then the sun disappeared, the sky became dark and a contingent of Ozarks' finest citizens dressed in coveralls and plaid shirts, flopped down on the bleacher seats behind the row of seats where we were seated.

The men were bearded as the town was engaged in a yearlong celebration of its upcoming 150 year anniversary.[12] Their presence, it seemed, sucked up all of the oxygen that we were breathing.

Dread was in the air, it dawned on us that this historic moment was not for us and we would have been better off reading about politics in the ivory towers of Tuskegee Institute than being in a football stadium outflanked by ten or more white men who came to support their segregationist governor for president of the United States of America.

I thought I was going to die, killed by a stark raving mad mob of racists, unwilling to accept students in their midst who simply wanted to witness this historic moment.

Then we saw a black man dressed in dark slacks, a tweed suit coat and tie. Unlike us and the white men in the crowd, he was clean shaven. He wore a mustache and a distinctive pin in his coat lapel. He made eye contact with us, which assured us that he was probably employed by the secret service, and that he was not going to allow anything evil to happen to us.

The dread I felt rescinded ever so slightly, Wallace's helicopter landed, he sauntered to the

---

[12] http://files.usgwarchives.org/al/dale/newspapers/gnw30earlyhis.txt

podium in command of his every step;[13] he was poised to be more than a spoiler in the 1972 Presidential contest. He gave a rousing speech full of code words and innuendos for his segregationist views. He told the crowd that there was "not a dime worth of difference between the Democratic Party and the Republican Party."

As Wallace closed out his speech, his supporters hollered, hooted, and jumped up and down; they were on cloud nine. Amid this euphoria we elected to take our leave. This proved to be extremely problematic as we had to walk through what seemed like a gantlet of white women, some with new born babies in their arms, they were all excited and not expecting any black people to be in the crowd, might they be careless and bump into one of us? In such a highly charged atmosphere, this could have led to a savage vigilante reaction.

We found our way to our car, still hungry; we drove through the night back to Tuskegee, not daring to stop for a comfort break or for food.

I called my mom the next morning, I cried out about babies being bred to hate me without ever meeting me. "How in heaven's name," I cried, "will people ever learn to live together?"

---

[13] In 1977, Wallace greeted me at Tompkins Hall on the Tuskegee campus quite differently, as he stopped the State Trooper who was pushing his wheel chair, to grasp my hand and said, "Good to see you." He was in Tuskegee to address the National Association of Black Manufacturers who was meeting on campus that year. In 1972 Wallace was shot by a gunman while making a campaign stop. His injuries left him unable to walk.

NJAKA'S BOLD MOVE

My two political science study buddies, Cheryl and Larry, studied hard, but had a difficult time corralling an "A" from Dr. Njaka. He, after, all had been a general in a deadly tribal war that pitted the oil-rich and Christian Igbo's against the Muslim slave traders who had sold the ancestors of Cheryl, Larry and I into enslavement in America.

Dr. Njaka was on a mission to train Africans in America to take charge of the political institutions which governed their lives. He was strict. We called him "Bones," behind his back, of course, because no calcified bone could be any harder than Dr. Njaka when it came to his kinsmen by default learning the American political system.

Looking out from behind his desk, the general could see just how far his countrymen had strayed from the cultural life of their tribal villages in West Africa after centuries of Americanization. I gathered from his lectures Dr. Njaka was disappointed in our journey.

With our eyes focused toward his desk as students, one sensed the global divide between Africans in the Diaspora and Africans on the continent.

There were, to be sure, African students on campus from practically every nation-state on the continent, but the only one we had any contact with was Dr. Njaka, Chair of the Political Science Department. We could not escape contact with him.

In the summer of 1971, while girding our loins to do battle with Dr. Njaka for another academic year, news came via Jet Magazine that "Bones" had accepted an offer to coordinate the Afro-American Studies Program at the University of Maryland.

The late 1960s saw a demand for Afro-American history courses from the radical left of the slower, yet steadily marching wing, of the civil rights movement. Several private universities moved swiftly to identify curriculums for their black students. Black students at Columbia and Cornell had locked the Trustees of their lofty universities in their board rooms until the schools agreed to include courses in Afro-American History.

The University of Maryland, Baltimore County resides just below the Mason-Dixon Line, yet it is essentially a slow walk into the District of Columbia perched on the shores of the Chesapeake Bay.

Thus it is not surprising that Maryland, the southern state which did not secede from the Union with other southern states, permitted its flagship university, or at least, the Baltimore County campus to offer Afro-American studies. It all came about when a group of faculty members and students in 1970 convinced the university that great benefit could come out of such a program.

The University of Maryland, Baltimore County, not only offered courses in African American Studies; it gave divisional status to this curriculum. A part of the core curriculum as designed by Njaka was a course in "White Studies," which Njaka defined as, "An examination of the essentially European culture which has dominated the non-white populations in the world over the past century."[14]

According to the Baltimore Afro-American, a year and a half after arriving at UMBC, Njaka had secured the approval from the Maryland Council of Higher education for a Bachelor of Arts degree in African American Studies. It would be the first time that Maryland had approved a curriculum leading to a Bachelor of Arts degree in African American studies in any school in the university system.[15]

This approval came at a time when most Southern universities were debating whether to open the admissions process to the great-grandsons and great-granddaughters of the nation's former enslaved people. Njaka's desire to put the "white man" under a microscope met with resistance and he left the division at the end of the 1973-74 academic years. His political science emphasis on blacks obtaining political power was replaced for that of a director with whose advanced academic degree was in sociology.

Thus, Njaka's idea to study white men was blunted in exchanged for more social welfare studies of the problems ingenious to the African American community. UMBC graduated its first Bachelor of Arts class in 1975 and by that time it

---

[14] Jet Magazine, August 12, 1971, P. 47
[15] Baltimore Afro-American, April 14, 1973, p. 38

had stripped the African American Studies of its Divisional status.

Shortly thereafter, Njaka took ill; his bold move had flickered robustly, and then died.

The District of Columbia, in the early 1970s, was heralded as a Mecca for African Americans. It took on the name of "Chocolate City" in the parlance of African American youth. The term was bandied about as freely as water cascading down a waterfall without so much as a whimper from anyone.

These were the days prior to political correctness entering the American lexicon. Men and women of all racial hues were free to express how they felt about an issue without anyone pulling the political correctness card. Besides that, Caucasian Americans paid very little attention to issues that concerned African Americans. So no one cared if blacks claimed the District as their "Chocolate City."

Back then, your point of view either lived or died on its own merits. In fact, political correctness is a form of a race card. I am not sure why black people embrace the term because it was designed by the larger culture to denigrate people who disagreed with their political point of view. These points of view seldom have little if anything at all to do with race.

Instead of retorting, "you are only saying that because I am black," it now becomes, "you are only saying that because you don't like gays or Christians or Democrats, etc."

In 2005, Ray Nagin, like me, a former student-athlete at Tuskegee University,[16] drew the ire of whites in his city when, as mayor of New Orleans, he suggested the Bush administration should send aid to his "Chocolate City" following the battering New Orleans took from the destructive winds of Hurricane Katrina.

Had Nagin lost his mind? A hip phrase in the 1970s was politically incorrect and insensitive in the new century. My, how time changes some things. While other things, tend to remain relatively the same.

Britt Lyle, a Florida lawyer and former collegiate classmate of Nagin, thinks Nagin is still paying for this politically incorrect gaffe.[17]

"No doubt Ray is paying for embarrassing the white overseers who did little to rescue people who were drowning in their attics because the federal government did not have a plan to get them off their roofs and out of their attics. He should have been given a great humanitarian medal, instead he gets prosecuted," Lyle said.

Nagin, an accounting major, was four years away from his arrival in Tuskegee when Dr. Njaka set out to establish and coordinate an Afro-American studies program at the University of Maryland. He missed the banter of Njaka pointing

---

[16] Nagin attended Tuskegee on a baseball scholarship from 1974-1978, while I was a walk-on both the 1972 and 1973 teams.
[17] In 2013 Nagin was convicted in federal court for bribery stemming from his management of federal funds to rebuild New Orleans following the Hurricane Katrina disaster. On July 8, 2014, Nagin was sentenced to 10 years in prison. He commences his prison term in September 2014.

out the insensitivity that black Americans showed to their African brothers, these discussions may have sensitized him to the cultural diversity of his New Orleans of the 21st century.

It was ironic that in the summer of 1971 Dr. Njaka left the historic campus at Tuskegee Institute to establish an African-American studies program at Maryland.

Paradoxically, as previously mentioned, "The Institute" had been organized on the suggestion of Lewis Adams, a Negro businessman. Yet Tuskegee Institute in 1971 did not have a Black Studies program and suppressed any discussion of Black Studies as an unnecessary academic discipline for the education of the American Negro in the last quarter of the 20th century.

In 1968, every single student at Tuskegee Institute was expelled from the school because of a student demonstration similar to those held at Columbia and Cornell (Tuskegee's Board of Trustees was locked up in Dorothy Hall for three days) demanding that the Institute create an Afro-American Studies program, among other issues.[18]

It would take an order from Judge Frank Johnson, sitting on the Federal District Court bench in Montgomery, Alabama to order the school to re-admit the expelled students.[19]

Clarence Jones, a pitcher on the Tuskegee baseball team, recalled being summarily

---

[18] http://www.southerncourier.org/lowres/Vol4_No17_1968_04_27.pdf

[19] Ibid

suspended from the school and having to reapply for admission.

"The baseball team had just arrived in Nashville, Tennessee to play a game against Fisk University, when Coach Bishop received a call from the school that told him the school was going to be shut down and that he was to suspend his road trip, bring the students back to campus so they could remove their property from their dorm rooms. When we arrived back in Tuskegee, the National Guard had the school locked down; I cleaned out my room and left the campus for home. I later got a letter from the school telling me I had to reapply for admission. I did and was accepted back in the school. The campus Photographer, P. H. Polk[20] took pictures of the protesters in Dorothy Hall and anyone who the administration could identify from the photographs was expelled. The students were able to get the American Civil Liberties Union involved in their case and all students were allowed back into the school."

Ironically, Polk's work, which is renowned for recording the illustrative history of Tuskegee and it visitors, over a 45 year period beginning in 1939, led to the expulsion of the entire Tuskegee Institute student body in 1968. After the court Federal Judge Frank Johnson ordered Tuskegee to readmit all students, they did then promptly expelled, Michael Wright, a student leader from Memphis, Tennessee. He was never allowed to return to Tuskegee.

---

[20] http://aafa.galileo.usg.edu/aafa/view?docId=ead/aarl96-014-ead.xml;query=;brand=default

The other ironic twist of fate is that the lawyer who represented Tuskegee Institute in federal court seeking to permanently ban each expelled student was Fred D. Gray, the fame civil rights attorney, who represented Rev. Martin Luther King, Jr. and Rosa Parks during the Montgomery Bus Boycott. Gray would also play a significant role in uncovering the Tuskegee Syphilis Experiment.

Tuskegee has a long history of summarily suspending bright students who question administrative decisions. This writer was suspended in 1973 for advocating that the school not deed certain properties over to the National Park Service in exchange for the Park Service to preserve and maintain certain buildings.

Those buildings were The Oaks (the residence of Booker T. Washington), the George Washington Carver Museum and Tompkins Hall, which housed the student cafeteria and student recreational facility. The Institute argued that the buildings were very old and as they aged the upkeep would be cost prohibited.

At twenty-years of age, I smelled a rat.

The Grey Columns, an ante-bellum mansion, which sits just outside the campus and owed by the Varner family, a Macon County, Alabama family with large land holdings dating back beyond the Civil War, was thrown in as part of a deal that would designate the Tuskegee buildings and the Grey Columns as a National Historical Site.

Over the course of the next 40 years, the Park Service convinced the university, during the Payton Presidency, to reclaim responsibility for Tompkins Hall, just before the roof on top of the 1905 structure collapsed, requiring the university to expend monies for major renovations to restore the building.

Also, during the Payton presidency, the Park Service swapped the Grey Columns for the Institute's presidential residence. Thus the university undertook the burden of maintaining a structure built in the early 1800s. Both moves defeated the initial intent to lessen the financial burden on the university by deeding certain properties to the National Park Service for their future maintenance and upkeep.

The school has continued its draconian measures into the twenty-first century. In 2014 Tuskegee amended the Student Handbook in the middle of the academic year to threats of suspension and expulsion for any student who uttered criticism of the university or any official at the university on social media. After a robust protest on social media from students, the university re-amended that section of the Student Handbook to prohibit cyber-bullying.

IGNORE THE RACE QUESTION, BUILD BUSINESSES AND A STRONG WORK ETHIC

Ninety years after its birth, Tuskegee focused its attention on business education. The school's first principal, Booker T. Washington founded the National Negro Business League in 1900. This organization preceded the United States Chamber of Commerce by twelve years.

Washington's idea for a National Negro Business League was a result of reading an article by the Harvard educated Dr. W. E. B. Dubois in the "Southern Workman."

Dubois researched the 1900 census data. He was perhaps the first scholar who tried to make sense out of this volume of data collected every ten years by the federal government. The data was clear that blacks were not advancing in business. Dubois pointed out this discrepancy in a piece he wrote in the "Southern Workman."

The "Southern Workman" had been founded by Samuel Chapman Armstrong, the Union General instrumental in the founding of Hampton Normal and Agricultural Institute, now known as Hampton University. Also, Armstrong recommended Booker T. Washington, a Hampton alumnus, to Lewis Adams and George Campbell as an excellent candidate to serve as the first principal of the Tuskegee Normal School.

When Washington came across Dubois' stark numbers, he had to one-up his intellectual adversary, so he posited that opening up businesses was a logical progression for a people one generation removed from slavery.

In 1971, on the heels of Dr. Njaka's departure from Tuskegee, Dr. Andrew Brimmer, then a governor in the Federal Reserve System and a member of the Tuskegee Board of Trustees said, "I believe those men and women who are convinced they can succeed in business should have a chance to try their luck."

By 1981 Dr. Brimmer served the nation as head of Federal Reserve and Chairman of the Tuskegee Board of Trustees. He relinquished the Tuskegee chairmanship in 2010. In 2007 Tuskegee University's commitment to business education was cemented with the dedication of the Andrew F. Brimmer College and Business Science building.

Ironically, Brimmer in his four-decade tenure on the Tuskegee Board and with his nationally recognized business acumen did not attempt to create an advanced degree in business. This gets to the nexus of what plagues African American communities in this country. There is never any attempt to capitalize upon the goodwill and legacy already achieved by institutions of black cultural development in America. We continue to re-create the wheel without moving forward.

I dare say, you could not find any Black Studies program on any Historically Black College or University campus in 1971.

Yet black scholars made a demand upon historically white colleges and universities to do what their black counterparts at Historically Black Colleges and Universities were either afraid to do or found counter-productive to the advancement of black culture.

However, Dr. Njaka was educated at the University of California at Los Angeles and had seen firsthand the politics of war. And no less a war than one led by a western interest anxious to get its hand on the oil fields of central Nigeria.

He was a bit more skeptical of the motivations of white people. Thus he believed it was important to study the white man. He told the editors at Jet Magazine in the summer of 1971:

"We haven't yet known the white man. We need to understand why the white man has been doing what he has been doing to us. This will enable us to reach a better compromise between races and an opportunity to live together as human beings. This has been my dream all along."[21]

Reading those words sitting on my mom's front porch in the summer of 1971 stunned me more than the exhilaration I felt knowing, just like that, in a twinkling of an eye, Dr. Njaka was out of our hair.

This army general from Biafra had the audacity to think the University of Maryland would be comfortable with a program that put the white man under a microscope.

Yet his philosophy when viewed from the prism of time continued that age old dichotomy presented by the Booker T. Washington statue which stands at the center of Tuskegee's campus: The dichotomy of accommodation versus full reconstruction into American society as equals.

---

[21] Jet Magazine, August 12, 1971, P. 47

Washington, in his nice Republican suit, exemplified the full reconstruction of the Negro into American society, and the kneeling farmer in his "up from slavery clothes," clutching his anvil, depicted the working class status the Negro was assigned in all things social. Ironies abound, as both Washington and the kneeling farmer were both born enslaved. While a few have been welcomed into the inner circle, the masses are left, to paraphrase the words of Washington "to pull themselves up by their own boot straps."

Dr. Andrew Brimmer, also spoke with the editors of Jet Magazine that summer. He told them that "their [Negroes] interest lies in the opening up of genuine employment opportunities and in accelerating occupational upgrading."

Brimmer's thoughts were echoed by Emory O. Jackson, the legendary managing editor of *The Birmingham World*. During the summer of 1971, Jackson posited:

"What I would like to suggest as measurement of change and progress is the spirit of Black youth. My observation has been that not many Blacks seem to be willing for economic adventure, the desire to build institutions, to invent opportunities."[22]

For the next four years, Jackson through his column in what his readers affectionately called *"The World,"* urged young people to get involved in economic adventures in the age of "affirmative action," then he transitioned, and I

---

[22] Jet Magazine, August 12, 1971, P. 34

found myself, a recent Tuskegee Institute graduate, living in his house, learning the newspaper trade and stumbling in his big shoes.

LOVE IS THE ANSWER

In the mid-west during the summer of 1971 at Northwestern University, Eva Jefferson, the first black president of the Student Government Association was taking the helm. She searched for an answer to the rage being expressed by black people who were trying to understand Viet Nam and the assassinations of Bobby Kennedy and Martin Luther King, Jr.

The antidote of black people in the parlance of the 1960s was to see all rightness in all things black and wickedness in all things white.

Perhaps this was necessary to throw off the shackles of centuries of mistreatment, and Ms. Jefferson was groping for a way to place into context the changing mood of black people toward the white privileged class.

"I could not resolve what to do with the white people who were my friends, because no matter how much I could hate a white face walking down the street, I couldn't hate those white people I had grown close to and no amount of rationalization could negate their basic good."[23]

Hers was an awakening. It was a realization

---

[23] Jet Magazine, August 12, 1971, P. 47

that black advancement could not be built upon hatred. There had to be some other reason to finally be free to move about the country and make use of any public accommodations available to other Americans and foreign visitors of the lighter races of humankind.

The hue and cry at the time was for "black power" and for black people to control the institutions in their lives; institutions built on racism and sustained by racism. It would take 36 years before another African American would be elected president of the Student Government Association at Northwestern University.

Could there have been such a vacuum of African American talent that it would cause a majority white student body to vote in a white member, or other non-black ethnic minority, year in and year out? Moreover, is this an important question in the 21st Century?

But, how long will it take to elect another African American President of the United States of America? Will other talented African Americans soon be given a chance to run the most powerful military industrial complex in the history of the world?

Perhaps these rhetorical questions beg the real question: Could these questions explain why every move made by President Obama is made to seem like it is the worst policy that anyone could have thought to enact?

THEY ALWAYS GET AWAY

I am not so sure that today's black people have a clear manifestation of their destiny. I am almost certain, that blacks have lost their identity. The melting pot continues to blend colors as it always has. Yet the game has changed, or at least the rules governing the game are changing.

The far right political sphere has turned the rules of engagement on their head by adopting the language of dissent from the civil rights movement. They have made it appear that there is an assault on the rights and privileges of the majority; just as the majority is quickly becoming the minority.

Thus, laws meant to protect blacks from white privilege, perhaps will soon prevent blacks from advancing, as the new white minority, argues the fairness of majority rule.

This in a nutshell is where the nation finds itself as America's first African president seeks re-election.[24] Already numerous states in the union have filed petitions in court challenging President Obama's right to be listed upon their state ballot in Democratic Primaries and the General Election.

This is a move, unprecedented in the annals of American Presidential Elections.

---

[24] This essay was written prior to the 2012 Presidential election

"Harold Michael Harvey, you know what the answer is," Kathy Bird, a Facebook friend penned the other day.

"The election of an African American president has torn the scab off of racial wounds... that continues to epitomize, and the nastiness underneath has been clearly exposed. Of course, normally, there are code words and other 'reasons' to feel or vote a certain way. It's the same old story, play the racial divide for all it's worth. It's almost too easy to make folks vote against their best interest."

Kathy Bird, if racial identity is important, is a white American, my age. We grew up in the same hometown, Macon, Georgia, attended high school during the tumultuous mid-1960s. She attended the predominately white female high school that was the sister school to the predominately white male high school I attended.

Because of the social mores of that time and space, we did not meet until a year ago courtesy of Mark Zuckerberg's Facebook and as of this writing have never shaken hands.

Of such is the historical backdrop occupying the difficult problem of Race in American society, both pre-Obama and perhaps, post-Obama?

"They always get away," Cheryl Lattimore called to say when George Zimmerman was issued a bond in the shooting death of a black Florida teenager, Trayvon Martin.

"When Zimmerman called the police he said, 'they always get away,' talking about black people, but you know white people always get away with murder. I don't think the young people today will take this injustice like we did," Cheryl said.

She was pointing out the frustration felt throughout black America on how the Trayvon Martin shooting was handled in Sanford, Florida, on February 26, 2012. Her hue and cry echoes those of Medgar Evers describing why he got involved in civil rights work back in 1963:

"It seemed that this (racism) would never change..."[25]

Cheryl's feelings and those of others are fueled by the constant attacks upon America's first president of color. All of which suggests, perhaps Dr. Njaka had the right idea: Someone should undertake to study the white man as a species to understand how and why he does what he does in questions of race and culture.

Alas, Frances Cress Welsing, has done just this very thing, researched and written about the need for cultural dominance in the white male species, in her seminal work, "The Cress Theory of Color Confrontation."

Perhaps, Cress Welsing's theory is faulty, but assuming she is correct, as with any illness, there can be no cure without the patient's

---

[25] "Medgar Evers". www.HistoryLearningSite.co.uk.web.

recognition of the problem. Hopefully, sometime between now and the dawning of the 22nd century there will have been that great recognition and much sought after cure.

Moreover, the institutions which primarily service the diverse community of African Americans must get back to the mission of teaching descendants of the formerly enslaved how to navigate in America, as America has come to be defined, in the 21st century.

This brief diatribe above on where Tuskegee University started out in the great mission to bring Africans out of enslavement and into full citizenship, coupled with the pettiness she has slipped into overtime; points out the fact that African Americans have lost their compass and are wandering in a changing America.

At the same time there is an organized movement based on race to turn the clock back to pre-Civil War America, by keeping black men in check with laws or guns or both; all made legal by a jury trial of one's peers; although one's peers may have fallen victim to their subconscious racial biases and prejudices.

If the 5th president of Tuskegee Institute could not adequately defend the name of the school to the 40th President of the United States, how does anyone expect twenty-something-year-old African Americans, who are devoid of a "Jim Crow" past, to understand the nuances of race when sitting in judgment of a trial that had its genesis in the racial conundrums of the street?

Moreover, if in 30 years, this same well-educated, college president did not maintain a sense of history and respect for the cultural legacy that he administered and resumed the burden of maintaining historical relics his predecessor had discarded, how can one expect young people like Trayvon Martin and Jordan Davis to realize the minefield their daily lives actually are?

Tuskegee Institute, Alabama
June 9, 2012

ESSAY 3

Zimmerman Not Guilty

"Fiat justitia ruat caelum – Let justice be done though the heavens falls."

Seneca, *"Piso's justice"*

George Zimmerman, the 29-year-old neighborhood watch coordinator who killed unarmed 17-year-old Trayvon Martin, has been found not guilty of second-degree murder and manslaughter by a jury of six women.

Zimmerman touched off national outrage and demonstrations last year when he squeezed off a single round from his handgun into Martin's chest. Martin had taken a break from watching the NBA All-Star game and walked to a nearby 7-Eleven store where he purchased an Arizona Ice Tea for himself and a bag of Skittles for his stepbrother.

The gunshot played over and over for the jury at the Zimmerman trial muted the cries for help of either Zimmerman or Martin. Witnesses battled over whose voice they heard crying out. The jury verdict settled that issue. It was George Zimmerman.

There was not a peep out of the jury for the first 13 hours after retiring to deliberate the fate of Zimmerman. Then, Judge Debra Nelson received a note from the jury asking for more clarification on the jury instruction on manslaughter. Judge Nelson wrote back that if they had a specific question she would answer it, but that the law prohibited her from responding to questions about the instructions in general.

On the night of the shooting, Zimmerman was taken into custody for questioning. He gave an oral and written account of his actions and thoughts leading up to, during, and after the shooting. He was released hours later in the early morning of the following day.

On the day of his release, he met again with investigators and provided them with a video walkthrough of the events that he alleged led up to pulling his gun from a concealed holster and shooting Martin in the heart.

Although Zimmerman did not take the witness stand in his own defense, his statements were introduced into evidence by the prosecution's team, which was led by Bernie de la Rionda.

In his closing argument, de la Rionda masterfully cross-examined the oral, written and video statements of Zimmerman. It was as if Zimmerman had actually taken the witness stand and was being confronted with his prior inconsistent statements.

Later, during the state's rebuttal, Assistant State Attorney John Guy told the jury those inconsistent statements were "lies" in answer to the defense's argument that Zimmerman had done nothing wrong in killing Martin.

But before we could get to Zimmerman's day in court, he first had to be arrested and charged. Former Sanford Police Chief Bill Lee was reluctant to press charges against Zimmerman. Lee's refusal led to nationwide demonstrations and calls for Lee's firing and the arrest of Zimmerman.

President Barack Obama got involved when questioned about the case at a press conference. He said, "If I had a son, he would look like Trayvon Martin."

Jeff Triplett, the Republican mayor of

Sanford, Fla., met with Martin's family and ordered the 911 audiotapes released to them. They were played in his office for Martin's mother and father. When the "Lauer 9-1-1"[26] call was played, the parents heard and shared the terror of Martin's last moments in life.

Triplett, many local observes believed, forced Chief Lee into retirement and the New Black Panther Party issued a "Wanted Dead or Alive" bounty on Zimmerman before an arrest warrant was issued by local authorities.

Republican Florida Governor, Rick Scott, stepped into the fray and appointed a special prosecutor to investigate this case. Scott appointed state attorney Angela Corey. Following her investigation, Corey had Zimmerman arrested and charged him with second-degree murder. At the time, critics were clamoring for a first-degree murder charge.

Following the close of the evidence in this case, many legal pundits believed that manslaughter would have been the more appropriate charge. The state was able to get Circuit Court Judge Debra Nelson to charge the jury to consider manslaughter as a lesser included offense of second-degree murder. Under Florida law, both offenses carry essentially the same punishment.

The trial was not a smooth one for the state. Their key witness, Rachel Jeantel was engaged in a cell phone conversation with Martin

---

[26] This name was used in court to identify the 9-1-1 call that came into the police department which was made by Zimmerman's neighbor, Ms. Lauer.

when Zimmerman caught up with him, at the now infamous T intersection. She did not perform well on her first day on the witness stand.

Although she recovered the second day, things continued to go awry for the state as their forensic witnesses; Dr. Valerie Rao and Dr. Shiping Bao did not come across as being very knowledgeable about their science.

The defense, led by veteran Florida lawyers Mark O'Mara and Don West, hammered away at the state's case from start to finish. They brought to the witness stand, over seven voice-recognition witnesses, who testified that the voice crying out for help on the "Lauer 9-1-1" call was Zimmerman.

O'Mara and West introduced testimony from weapons and police procedure experts to explain the Florida self-defense law. O'Mara argued in closing that Zimmerman was within his legal rights to shoot and kill Martin.

In the end, prosecutor John Guy brought us the 21st century equivalent to Johnnie Cochran's "If the gloves don't fit, you have to acquit," when he said: "To the living we owe respect. To the dead we owe the truth."

Guy left a parting shot with Zimmerman when he said: "Trayvon Martin may not have had George Zimmerman's blood on his hands, but George Zimmerman will forever have Trayvon Martin's blood on his hands."

Sanford, Florida
July 13, 2013

ESSAY 4

Simmering with Zimmerman: James Baldwin's 'The Fire Next Time' revisited

"God gave Noah the rainbow sign, no more water, the fire next time!"

James Baldwin, "The Fire Next Time"

In 1963, James Baldwin penned his seminal work on race relations in America, "The Fire Next Time,"[27] two essays which served as a prophetic warning to his countrymen.

Just as the Hebrew Prophet Obadiah had warned of the destruction of Edom, Baldwin, according to the New York Times, "brilliantly with searing penetration masterfully" laid out the case for America's doom if the nation did not get a handle on the "Negro Problem."

The first essay, "My Dungeon Shook: Letter to My Nephew on the One Hundredth Anniversary of the Emancipation," was originally published in The Progressive, Madison, Wisconsin. The second essay, "Down at the Cross," originally appeared in The New Yorker under the title, "Letter from a Region in my Mind."

The book's prelude and its last sentence end in a song first uttered by a slave:

"God gave Noah the rainbow sign, no more water, the fire next time!"

Baldwin's refrain sparked the battle cry of the 1960s, *"Burn, baby, burn,"* as American urban centers - Los Angeles (Watts), Detroit, Cleveland (Hough), Tampa, Newark, Buffalo, Chicago and the District of Columbia - went up in flames.

An expatriate living in the South of France at the time of the 1963 March on Washington, Baldwin was initially denied a visa to enter the

---

[27] The Fire Next Time, Dell Publishing House, Inc., 1963

country because Attorney General Bobby Kennedy and presumably President John F. Kennedy did not want him to speak at the march now made famous by Rev. Dr. Martin Luther King Jr.'s "I Have a Dream" speech.

The following year, these two essays were published under the title, "The Fire Next Time."

In "My Dungeon Shook," Baldwin had that same conversation with his nephew that mothers, fathers and uncles in the African American community have been having with their male kin since the dawning of the Trans-Atlantic Slave Trade. This conversation is not a rite of passage, but a rite of survival.

In 1963, it was no less difficult for Baldwin - he started his letter five times, tearing each of them up before finding the right words[28] - than it was for my grandmother to have that conversation with me in 1955, or the conversation I had with my son in 1993, or the same conversation going on across African American communities in 2013, in light of the killing of Trayvon Martin.

"You can only be destroyed," Baldwin tells his nephew, also named James Baldwin, "by believing that you are what the white world calls a nigger. I tell you this because I love you, and please don't you ever forget it."[29]

"And I know," Baldwin writes, "...this is the crime of which I accuse my country and my countrymen, and for which neither I nor time

---

[28] Ibid, P. 17
[29] Ibid, P. 18

nor history will ever forgive them, that they have destroyed and are destroying hundreds of thousands of lives and do not know it and do not want to know it....But it is not permissible that the authors of devastation should also be innocent. It is the innocence which constitutes the crime."[30]

In making clear the caste system that his nephew was born into, Baldwin speaks of the plight of every African born in America. "You were born where you were born and faced the future that you face because you were black and *for no other reason*."[31]

Baldwin then gives the young Mr. Baldwin (his nephew), a template for survival in America. "There is no reason for you to try to become like white people and there is no basis whatever for their impertinent assumption that *they* must accept *you*. The really terrible thing, old buddy, is that you must accept *them*. And I mean that very seriously. You must accept them and accept them with love."[32]

Baldwin, as has every responsible African American adult before him and those after him, ended this rite of survival clearly spelling out the status of the American Negro, "You know, and I know, that the country is celebrating one hundred years of freedom one hundred years too soon. We cannot be free until they are free..."[33]

---

[30] Ibid, P. 18, 19
[31] Ibid, P. 21
[32] Ibid, P. 22
[33] Ibid, P. 24

The jury verdict in the George Zimmerman murder trial punctuates the fact that a celebration of 150 years of freedom this year, 2013, is 150 years too soon.

In the second essay, "Down at the Cross," Baldwin wrestles with the concept of America as a Christian nation.

He points out the paradox and myths of this position. In it, he cites Rudyard Kipling to inspire African Americans to *"Take up the White Man's burden-...,"* but only after he had carefully dissected the diabolical hell that whites had built for the formerly enslaved. "..., White people, who had robbed black people of their liberty and profited by this theft every hour that they lived, had no moral ground on which to stand. They had the judges, the juries, the shotguns, the law-in a word, power."[34]

Feeling lost in the wilderness, Baldwin left the church where he had been since becoming a child preacher at the tender age of 14. "Therefore, when I faced a congregation," Baldwin wrote, "it began to take all the strength I had not to stammer, not to curse, not to tell them to throw away their Bibles and get off their knees and go home and organize for example, a rent strike."[35]

Overcome with the indifference that white Christians showed towards the plight of black people, Baldwin posited, "If the concept of God has any validity or any use, it can only be to

---

[34] Ibid, P. 37
[35] Ibid, P. 53

make us larger, freer, and more loving. If God cannot do this, then it is time we got rid of him."

This juxtaposition pushed him out of the church and led Baldwin to accept an invitation to dine with the Honorable Elijah Muhammad, the leader of the Nation of Islam. Muhammad, a messenger of Allah, had just pulled off a coup. He had converted the heavyweight Champion of the World, Cassius Clay, to Islam and was looking to bring into the fold the literary genius of James Baldwin.

Although Baldwin railed against the vagaries the white dominance of society caused, he had far too many white friends he did not wish to alienate. Joining the Nation of Islam was not the answer that Baldwin was seeking to address the systemic and institutional racism he found in the country.

Muhammad preached that the black God was all set to destroy America in 1913, but extended its supremacy to give black people a chance to separate from white America. "Time," Baldwin reasoned in 'The Fire Next Time,' "...gets its teeth into doctrines and rends them... it destroys doctrines by proving them to be untrue." Then, 100 years later, in 2013, the leader of the Nation of Islam, the Honorable Louis Farrakhan , embraced the Christian God, Jesus, "as the only prophet that is coming back."

Consequently, understanding Baldwin's prophesy, "a hundred years after his technical emancipation, he [the American Negro] remains - with the possible exception of the American Indian - the most despised creature in his country," Farrakhan bridged the gap between blacks, who continued to opt for the Christian faith in larger numbers than any other faith, with the faith of black Muslims in America.

Until a year and a half ago, Zimmerman did not cast much of a shadow on the affairs of humankind. All that changed Feb. 26, 2012 when Zimmerman, profiled an African American teenager walking in his condominium community, stalked him, and baiting the youngster into fighting his way home.

Zimmerman then took his concealed weapon from his holster and shot the black teenager in the chest, killing him almost instantly.

A jury of five white women and one Latina woman gave more deference to the white/Latino defendant who testified through his inconsistent statements than to the young black lady, Rachel Jeantel, who was on the telephone with Trayvon Martin just moments before he was killed.

Baldwin laid out the precipice for the Zimmerman jury verdict 50 years ago. Their verdict was predictable. Nothing has changed how white people view black young men in this country.

Notwithstanding the presence of a black man in the White House, perhaps the only thing that has changed is the distain and disrespect with which the country now views its president.

Rev. Al Sharpton, president and founder of the National Action Network, called for rallies in 100 cities on the seventh day after the Florida jury released George Zimmerman with his gun.

Rage over Zimmerman is simmering in the countryside. It is quiet, deliberate, calculating and in little over a month, a coalition of progressive Americans will re-enact the March on Washington 50 years after King's dream. A dream once syrupy sweet was left to rot in the orange groves of Florida last week.

The nation's black citizens are often left out of the American dream. They sense their status is changing back to the forgotten Americans. With recent Supreme Court rulings on affirmative action and voting rights, black people are simmering over the acquittal of Zimmerman.

There is an African Spring coming to America. A non-violent, but a determined African Spring resolve not to stop until the denigrating narrative some white Americans hold in their minds about African Americans has been neutralized by laws or political muscle, or both.

Otherwise, Baldwin's words cry out from his tomb in the South of France, "If we do not now dare everything, the fulfillment of that prophecy, re-created from the Bible in song by a slave, is upon us: *'God gave Noah the rainbow sign, no more water, the fire next time.'*"

Sanford, Florida

July 18, 2013

ESSAY 5

Obama's Soul on Ice: A week later and I'm still numb

"How far in a state can a recognized moral wrong safely be compromised?"

> W. E. B. Dubois, "The Suppression of the African Slave-Trade to the United States of America, 1638-1870.

When the jury verdict was read in Sanford, Fla., last week, it jolted the nerve endings in my spinal cord, rendering me numb. A week after a jury of George Zimmerman's peers let him get away with killing a high school student in cold blood, I'm still numb.

I am numb not because Zimmerman was not found guilty of something; I'm numb over the fact that five white women and one Latina woman would put their racial feelings above doing the right thing.

One can argue as much as one pleases that such is the rule of law and the Zimmerman jury followed the instructions given to them by Judge Debra A. Nelson.

Nevertheless, I will always contend this jury reached its verdict based upon the racial biases they brought into the courthouse with them the morning they began their sequestered jury service.

This is precisely what their jury oath says they should not do. They are sworn to let their verdict speak the truth of what happened in the event before them.

If juror number B37's mental thought processes, as reflected in recent television news interviews on CNN, are any indication of those of the other five, then it comes as no surprise that the panel tended to give more credence to the White/Latino defendant than it did to three black witnesses who testified against Zimmerman's version of what happened that night.

In a word, the verdict is legal, but, I dare say, not just. They (white people who kill black people) seem to, "always get away."

Last week President Barrack Obama talked about the historical prism through which black people see the Zimmerman trial. He called upon the nation to open up and have an honest dialogue on race. He has given such speeches before on this issue.

The first was in 2008, when, as seen from the black prism of history, white racists forced him to cut ties with his preacher, Rev. Dr. Jeremiah A. Wright, Jr., over sermons Wright had given 20 years *before* Obama decided to run for president. Obama's rhetoric distanced him from the man who had brought him to Christ, baptized and married him.

He apologized to white Americans for Wright's Afro-centric world view of history. It brought him some breathing room and his campaign stayed alive.

Later in 2008, he gave another race speech after a firestorm sprang up in Pennsylvania over his remarks that "whites clung to their guns and religion." This speech set Obama apart from other black leaders as he wove blacks and whites into the tapestry of the American fabric in a way no one had done since Abraham Lincoln. It soothed the conscience of white voters caught up in "hope and change."

Finally, a black man to whom whites could give their vote -- he won!

Conservative whites swallowed hard with what I perceive as subconscious racial guilt. There was no need to fret over civil rights any longer. The nation had turned a corner white conservatives were quick to proclaim.

Any talk of civil rights and whites accused blacks of playing the race card. No more listening to Rev. Jesse Jackson and Rev. Al Sharpton. "What more do the coloreds want?" This seemed to be the postulation after Obama's victory.

Black Americans were willing to play along with this jig. After all a brother, his wife and kids were in the White House.

Meanwhile, black issues went unresolved as Tea Party Republicans pushed to elect right wing conservatives to redress their agenda to congress and gays got the right to marry from the Supreme Court.

The same court, a week earlier, had weakened voting rights and affirmative action laws which favored black Americans. It seemed that the points of view, of all ethnic and cultural groups in America were advancing their interests, but African Americans.

Then a non-black jury in Florida listened to the history of the racial divide in the country, and broke the spirit of parents whose son died of a bullet wound to his chest. Their verdict stuck a dagger into the collective heart of African Americans.

Seemingly, at this point, Obama had had enough of the jig. In a press briefing last Friday

(July 19, 2013), he put the onus square on the shoulders of white Americans to begin honestly seeking to heal racial wounds brought on by the history of whites and blacks in the United States of America.

National thought leaders Dr. Boyce Watkins and Tavis Smiley have assailed the president for taking too long in his administration to get to the "nitty gritty" of racial problems in the country. Both men wonder why it took President Obama so long to speak about race from the perspective of African Americans. Their criticism fails to account for the fact, that it does not matter how long, nor who prodded him, but the inescapable fact that he did.

Now that the president has opened the door, the ball is in white America's court.

Will whites begin the painful discussion to reconcile the problems of color that our joint history demands?

Will media executives begin to change the narrative of how they portray African Americans on the news and in television shows?

Will Hollywood produce and reward films that highlight the best in African American culture?

Obviously, to ask these questions is to point out how sad a perception whites have of blacks; yet it points us toward a solution to the problem of the color line.

Paraphrasing Dr. Martin Luther King Jr. speaking at the Riverside Church in New York on the Viet Nam War shortly before he met a sniper's bullet: "If America doesn't do something and do something in a hurry, I'm sorely afraid that we won't be here much longer."

Blacks have always been willing to discuss racial issues from their perspective of history. While whites, (feeling uncomfortable with the subject or simply feeling there is no need for such a discussion), have not been willing to engage in honest dialogue. Whereas black people have equality to gain whites fear losing the privilege of white skin.

The time is upon us to set at the table of brother-hood and learn how to live together as "one nation under God, indivisible, with liberty and justice for all."

If we do not dare try honest dialogue, all else is cheap window dressing and will doom any initiatives to bring the country with all of its ethnic and cultural groups together in the spirit of good old American democracy.

Washington, D. C.
July 21, 2013

ESSAY 6

Whites are dodging Obama's call for an honest discussion on race

> "Most white people hate Black people. The reason that most white people hate Black people is because whites are not Black people. If you know this about white people, you need know little else. If you do not know this about white people, virtually all else that you know about them will only confuse you."
>
> Neely Fuller, "The United Independent Compensatory Code/System/Concept: a textbook /workbook for thought, speech and/or action for victims of racism (white supremacy," 1969

Shortly after the 19th century ended, Dr. W. E. B. Dubois opined that, "the problem of the 20th century will be the problem of the color line, the relation of the lighter races of men to the darker races in Asia, Africa and the islands of the seas."

More than 60 years after uttering that prediction, Dubois closed his eyes in Accra, Ghana, on the day his countrymen had that great march on the mall in Washington. The day Dr. Martin Luther King, Jr., urged his fellow Americans to usher in a day when people will "be judged by the content of their character rather than by the color of their skin."

Not much had changed in those first 63 years. Albeit, black men in America had fought in three wars, learned to fly fighter planes in World War II, saved the agriculture of the South, separated blood plasma and created the concept of a blood bank.

Nevertheless very little changed in the relationship of the lighter races of men to the darker races.

Achievements by African Americans have never been the key to being judged by the content of their character. Black men and women were making tremendous advancements in science, arts and culture prior to both Dubois' and King's utterances.

Those advancements did not stop whites from segregating, nor enacting laws (vagrancy laws have their roots in post-Civil War America) that were enforced primarily against the men in the segregated black communities.

Neither did those achievements encourage whites, in large numbers, to welcome their black neighbors into fellowship with them on Sunday mornings.

The notion that blacks could achieve a modicum of respectability by modifying their behavior to "mainstream" standards is not a novel idea, CNN's Don Lemon, notwithstanding.

In the early 1900s, Booker T. Washington, from his leadership role at Tuskegee Institute, gave required lectures on Sunday evenings in the old Tuskegee Chapel on" character building."

In 1905, 10 years after "Plessey v. Ferguson" which legalized segregation, a number of these lectures were published in a book which bears the title, *"Character Building."*

In it, Washington urged blacks a generation removed from slavery to keep their communities clean, dress well, speak proper English and learn a useful trade, an idea that he espoused in his book *"Working with the Hands."*

Washington honestly believed that good character was the key to descendants of former slaves being accepted by the descendants of former slave owners, or those who had gained a certain privilege from white skin as a result of the economic system of slavery in the Americas.

Dubois, a man of high character and intellect, believed that character alone did not lead to acceptance by whites and that blacks, now freed from bondage, had to agitate for inclusion in the American dream.

Both stratagems were utilized in the 20th century.

In 1965, Dr. King's Selma-to-Montgomery march for voting rights shook the walls of second-class citizenship and the ballot, once denied to blacks in wholesale numbers, was now protected.

In 1976, 11 years after President Lyndon B. Johnson signed the 1965 Voting Rights Act, hands that had once picked cotton helped pick the 39th president (Jimmy Carter) of the United States.

During the 1970s, there was a commitment in the country to level the playing field by providing minorities an opportunity to participate in employment and in the procurement of goods and services in the federal system.

Most state and local governments followed suit.

Through the agitation of Rev. Jesse Jackson, many corporate entities created affirmative action plans that for the first time gave black Americans a chance for employment and business opportunities.

Because black parents on a large scale had insisted their children speak proper English, dress well and go to college there was a readily available pool of African Americans to accommodate the affirmative action scheme.

Things were changing; blacks in large numbers were becoming upwardly mobile for the first time in American history.

Whites began to push back. They argued that affirmative action was unfair to white people and it had to go. A great deal of resentment developed between whites and blacks in the workplace.

For the first time, for a generation of whites, the advantage of living in the same segregated communities and attending the same segregated churches and social clubs did not equate to promotion on the job.

Their anguish spilled over at home and their children, who now were forced to attend school with blacks - some of whom were bused into black neighborhoods to attend school - felt the control of their lives being eroded just to accommodate the blacks. White students pushed back until they either finished school or enough "Christian schools" could be built to get them out of the public school system.

Herein is the problem. The nation's first 74 years as a constitutional government bound whites and blacks together in the caste system of slavery, with whites being the masters and blacks the servants.

As a nation these past 150-plus years, we were hurled headlong into this struggle for equality by black people. Although laws have been enacted to facilitate this one-nation-under-God concept, those laws have accompanying social pains that neither time nor character building has been able to smooth out.

This brings us to the president's heartfelt belief, that he shared a couple of weeks ago (July

13, 2013). Obviously, the president did not speak to the White House press corps so he could tell African Americans that they needed to honestly have a discussion on race. He knows that blacks' perception of the problem will not change the dynamics of race in America; only a discussion among white people can do that.

Thus far white Americans have remained strangely silent in this race debate. The only ones who have ventured out into the discussion are conservatives like Bill O'Reilly. He is joined by several black conservatives who point fingers at the blacks who do not comport themselves as the conservatives think mainstream Americans should - as if the small segment of young black males who wear baggy pants is the sum total of a whole race of people.

Then the progressive news commentator, Don Lemon, weighed in on the topic to agree with O'Reilly and his band of conservatives, by metaphorically pulling out his Booker T. Washington list for character building.

Lemon, one of the few black commentators to survive the recent purge of black journalists at CNN, though well intentioned has managed to draw the ire of black thought leaders for suggesting that young black males should have more self-respect for themselves than he sees in the manner in which they dress and the language they speak.

Don Lemon's longtime friend and MSNBC commentator, Goldie Taylor, tweeted out over the weekend about his comments. Taylor called Lemon a "turncoat mofo," an acronym for an expletive which expressed otherwise would have to be edited out of this piece.

All of these discussions have obscured the intent of the President's suggestion to have an honest rap on race.

If the problem of the color line is ever to show improvement, it will only happen when white Americans collectively begin to have that painful discussion about race in America. Should they feel a need to point a finger at the blacks, then they ought to take careful stock of the four fingers pointing back in their direction.

Tuskegee Institute, Alabama

July 30, 2013

ESSAY 7

The killings of Trayvon Martin and Jordan Davis: More creepy white crap

> "Today we are witnessing a more subtle systemic approach to white genetic survival. The destruction of Black males now is indirect, so that the Black male victims themselves can be led to participate in – and then be blamed for – their own mass deaths."
>
> Dr. Frances Cress Welsing,
> "The Isis Papers:
> The Keys to the Colors," 1992

As a writer and former trial lawyer of some note a decade ago, there are a number of ways I could approach a piece on what I have learned from the killings of Trayvon Martin and Jordan Davis. I am going to ramble for a while and come back to two adjectives that stand out from both trials.

The first is "creepy white ..." from the George Zimmerman trial. You know the rest of that verbiage, but for my purposes there is no need to mention it here.

The other adjective is "... crap," from the Michael Dunn trial.

For my purposes I am going to substitute Dunn's characterization of Davis' music with the word white, as in "white crap." More specifically, as in what was in Dunn's mind the day he pulled out his gun and killed Jordan Davis.

Before I was 10 years old, my granddad, Charles Harvey, taught me how to track and trap wild game.

He taught me how to look down the barrel of a gun, align my nose with the sight at the tip of the barrel of a .22 caliber rifle and squeeze a single round. If you wanted that quail for supper, you only got one shot to get it before the flock fled the sound of gunfire.

He taught me three important things about guns: (1) How to clean them, (2) never to pick up a gun unless I planned to use it; and (3) that a dead man on the other end of a gun barrel can't talk.

The effective use of guns and gun safety

was taught as a rite of passage in the Deep South of my youth. Black boys were also taught how to outflank white hunters when they were encountered in the same hunting area. White hunters tended to think and act like they had first dibs on any wild game in the area. So I was taught to never be caught inside the perimeter where white hunters were tracking game as white hunters tended to think they had a right to shoot any target on the other end of their barrel, whether it was wild game or a ten-year-old Negro hunter.

These survival skills were taught to black boys growing up in the Jim Crow South. But then something happened after blacks began to celebrate being the first to live in a previously all-white neighborhood, or attend a previously all-white school, or work in a job previously reserved for whites, or to date a white girl or boy.

Many black parents stopped teaching survival skills. They were free at last, many thought. So survival skills gave way to teaching the young that they had a right to all the privileges and immunities appertaining to American life.

Scant attention was paid by black people to the fierce resistance in Boston, Charlotte, and Jacksonville. Indeed, all over the country the rights of blacks were being forced on a white population that had grown accustomed to the spoils of privilege. Whites fought back.

White private schools, many claiming to be "Christian schools," sprang up around the country to keep the races from mixing and getting to know each other on a human level.

White males who heretofore could command the best jobs in their local communities on the strength of their high school diplomas now found themselves the odd men out as affirmative action programs increasingly overlooked them for college-educated black men.

Affirmative action advancements caused the resentment to grow into a callous on the souls of anti-integration white males. They saw their ability to control the politics of their lives dipped into the melting pot that guaranteed the rights of minorities to enjoy the American dream.

God only knows what was taught about race relations in those private so called "Christian schools." We are now confronted with two generations of white men educated in these schools since the "freedom of choice" era (1964-1970) in American education.

Last year I attended a "no more names rally against gun violence" at the Georgia State Capitol. The rally was sponsored by "Mayors against Illegal Guns."

At this rally, I met Jordan's father, Ron Davis. He struck me as a good father who will never get over the loss of his son to such a senseless act of violence. I cannot fathom any mother or father who would be able to do so in similar situations.

I was also struck by the sheer number of guns that showed up at this anti-gun violence rally. The non-gun toting demonstrators were surrounded by white men carrying guns of all sizes and descriptions. Some of these men were private citizens promoting a healthy respect for the Second Amendment. Others were capitol police, all of whom were stationed at the front of the demonstrators and none positioned to keep the two groups separate.

Suddenly, the sage advice of Charles Harvey from five decades ago prompted me to out-flank the white men toting guns. I was inside the perimeter sandwiched between the gun-toting cops and the gun-toting counter-demonstrators. It was time to leave this gathering as it was no longer safe to be among the members of the "Mayors against Illegal Guns" group.

In order to leave, I advanced towards the outer-perimeter; where the private gun enthusiasts were positioned, a young white male with a gun on his hip challenged my position. He began to speak, I quickly stepped to my left and moved behind him; then asked him how he was doing. He had to awkwardly turn to face me. I had outflanked him before he knew it; he then gave me some verbiage that made it seem as if he was doing 100 percent better than me on my best day.

As I walked down the steps of the State Capitol, I watched his terrified eyes follow me over his right shoulder. I could see the fear in his eyes; feel the fear in the rise and fall of his chest. The confrontation he wanted from the Negro walking amid all the guns as if he was free was avoided. I walked down Central Avenue to my car and wrote my story on the rally.

Civil rights gains notwithstanding, it is plain to see the war for full citizenship wages on.

African American families have to get back to teaching their pre-teenage children survival skills.

Never grow tired of telling the children and grandchildren how we survived the Middle Passage, slavery, Jim Crow, crack-cocaine, voter disenfranchisement in the age of Obama and "stand your grounds" laws.

Don't forget to tell them that there are good white people who have helped us move from enslavement into freedom. Tell the children to continue to nurture the relationships that have been built up over time with good people whose skin just happened to be white. Also, tell them that there is a being called "creepy white crap," which needs to be avoided and outflanked at every turn. And please don't forget to tell them, that in a court of law, "a dead man on the other side of a gun barrel cannot talk."

Jacksonville, Florida
February 16, 2014

ESSAY 8

How can a black juror not see race in the loud-music trial?

"We are never completely contemporaneous with our present. History advances in disguise; it appears on stage wearing the mask of the preceding scene, and we tend to lose the meaning of the play. Each time the curtains rises, continuity has to be re-established. The blame, of course is not history's, but lies in our vision, encumbered with memory and images learned in the past. We see the past superimposed on the present, even when the present is a revolution."

Regis Debray,
"Revolution in the
Revolution?"1967

Race, according to Creshuna Miles, "was never brought up." Miles is Juror No. 8 in the Michael Dunn murder trial, also known as the loud-music trial.

I've never sat on a jury. I've been summoned several times to appear. On one occasion, the county sheriff sent the S.W.A.T. out to escort me to jury duty. On another occasion, I endured the jury-selection process in a death-penalty murder trial.

On the occasion of the death-penalty murder trial, I was a personal injury lawyer and I looked like a safe bet for both the state and the defense to explain the intricacies of the law to fellow jurors. Then the question arose about whether anyone had ever had a bad experience with law enforcement. My hand went up.

A deputy sheriff in plain clothes had come out to my home in his personal vehicle, without a warrant, and ordered me to get into his vehicle. When I asked for proof of a warrant, he could not produce one, so I declined his invitation and walked back inside my home.

This was in the spring of 1977, during the early days of the "Atlanta Missing and Murdered Children" mystery. At that time very little was printed in the Atlanta newspapers about the disappearance of these young black males.

All anyone knew about the disappearance of these young people was clouded in rumors. So I was not going to take a chance that the white man of fifty or sixty years was not intent on abducting me from my own driveway.

I defied his command. He reached for his gun, and before he could pull it out of his holster, I shouted at him, "I'm going inside my house and you are not going to shoot me."

He called out the boys. It was about to get ugly until my dad came home for lunch, something he seldom did.

Later, the judge explained that a summons had been sent for me to appear for jury duty on that date. I did not receive the summons, so I went to work as usual that morning and only happen to take a couple of co-workers home for lunch because they were curious what type of fare did a vegetarian eat.

I hired Bob Steele, an old lawyer, who monitored civil rights cases for the American Civil Liberties Union in Macon, Bibb County, Georgia. We settled the case out of court the very next day.

Suddenly, the mild-mannered personal injury lawyer did not look so good to the prosecution and I was struck from the panel.

So I do not know what jurors do when they do what they do.

As a former trial lawyer, I have picked at least 60 juries, five of which were for death-penalty murder cases.

I've always been mystified, if not mortified, every time a jury came back with a verdict. When they voted for my client and when they did not, I could never discern how they got through the process with their verdict.

When things go horribly wrong in our

society involving members of different ethnicities, race is always a factor. No matter how we want to spin it, race trumps everything.

Racism is not the overt outburst, which says, for instance, I'm going to shoot you because you are black. That was how it was done in yesteryear when whites had the color of law on their side.

Since the 1970s, racism is more covert. It is shaped by the perceptions people tend to have about those who are not in their ethnic group.

What possessed Michael Dunn to think that he could order a carload of African American teenagers to turn their music down?

I submit it is the same thing, omnipotent white skin, which told the Bibb County, Ga., deputy sheriff in 1977 he could order a black reporter into his vehicle without proof of his authority.

I resisted. He became violent and called in the S.W.A.T. to bring me in dead or alive. I avoided sure death when my father came home for lunch and begged them not to tear his door down.

Not much in racial perceptions changed between 1977 and 2012.

"Get in the car," the unidentified deputy commanded me.

"Turn that music down," Dunn commanded the carload of black teenagers.

"I'm going back in my house and you are not going to shoot me," I said to the unidentified deputy as he reached for his gun.

"I'm tired of people telling me what to do," Jordan Davis said to Michael Dunn.

"Are you talking to me," Dunn said to Davis.

Both white men had their authority questioned by black men half their age. So they overreacted the exact same way. Both resorted to overkill, the progeny of rage fueled by wounded racial feelings.

The deputy called in reinforcements to take me by force, while Dunn reached into his glove box, retrieved his gun and fired 10 times toward Davis and his friends.

But for the grace of God, I would not have lived to tell this story. I shudder to think of what lie the deputy would have told to justify killing an unarmed 24-year-old black newspaper reporter who did not have a criminal record.

Miles thinks that anyone who sees race in the killings of Jordan Davis needs "to get knowledgeable about the law."

I think the 21 year old Miles should get knowledgeable about American history, with a special concentration in African American history, because matters of race are not taught in American history.

You cannot get to justice in cases like the killing of Trayvon Martin and Jordan Davis without understanding the solemnity of race in America.

Moreover, it is four decades past time for African American parents to insist that school districts stop the bull and get serious once again about educating our children.

Otherwise, the complex dichotomy of race in the 21st century will be left to be defined by the Rachel Jeantel's and Creshuna Miles' meandering willy-nilly in the Diaspora.

Jacksonville, Florida

February 21, 2014

ESSAY 9

The Jury System Was Designed For Europeans To Judge Europeans

"Meanwhile millions of Negroes suffered lives of humiliation for five or six or more decades under a Jim Crow, white supremacist Constitution, because the Court betrayed the intent of the Reconstruction Amendments, emasculating, in particular, the privileges and immunities clause of the Fourteenth Amendment... And how many thousands of cases of miscarriage of justice have there been, for both Negro and white defendants in criminal cases, because the Court took half a century to begin reforming and civilizing state criminal procedures under the Fourteenth Amendment?"

Leonard W. Levy, Ph. D.
"Judgments: Essays on American Constitutional History," 1972

The Constitution of the United States of America, Amendment VI, grants the criminally accused a right to a "speedy and public trial ... by an impartial jury in the state and district where the crime shall have been committed."

The framers of the Constitution included this protection because of the brutal system in England where a person could be thrown into a dungeon without formal charges and tried before the crown without the benefit of a public trial or having people from the community hear the evidence against them.

To remedy this abuse of King George's government, the newly formed government in America granted its citizens a right to a trial by people in the community.

This 18th century concept was a vast improvement from what had been the plight of the criminally accused.

The system worked fine until the second American Revolution (also known as the Civil War) ended in 1865 with the freeing of the Africans who were enslaved in the United States.

Prior to this time, the courts were reserved for Europeans who judged other Europeans. The enslaved Africans were at the mercy of their captors.

The law of the land allowed every enslaver to deal with his captives as he pleased. There was very little if any justice for the enslaved.

After 1865, Africans living in America as citizens were granted access to the courts via

Section 1981 of the Civil Rights Act of 1866. If accused of a crime, these new citizens had the protection of the Sixth Amendment.

How that played out in real time is that jury service was reserved for landowners. In the late 18th and much of the 19th centuries, land ownership was mostly reserved for white men.

Thus, white men determined the fate of Africans accused of crimes in America for most of their first 100 years of freedom from bondage.

Clearly, the "jury of your peers" enacted in its pristine form by the framers worked when European men judged European men. The empirical data or evidence tended toward guilt or innocence. This is as it should be.

This system became skewed when Africans were brought before the courts. Often they were tried without benefit of other Africans being on the jury, as landownership was reserved for white men.

When white women came into ownership of land -- for instance, through inheritances -- the requirement for jury service was changed from the landed gentry to permit only those who were found on the voter rolls to serve on juries. White women were not allowed to vote until 1920.

For 13 years following the revolution waged by the Southern states, Africans living in America who owned land had access to the voter rolls. Yet, seldom were any called for jury duty.

Thus, criminal justice in America has from Day one been a system designed to protect the interests of white men, poor white women did not figure into the system until women began burning their bras in the 1970s.

Whenever African Americans come before the system, the races of the parties involved have always been the tipping point in deciding which side gets the benefit of the doubt.

For instance, Trayvon Martin does not get the benefit of the doubt that he had a right to walk home without being stalked and baited into fighting by a white man.

Jordan Davis does not get the benefit of the doubt that he had a right to disregard a command to turn his music down without being shot to death by a white man.

In each instance, a white man was the aggressor who initiated the deadly altercation.

The George Zimmerman and Michael Dunn trials are modern-day examples of how justice has played out in American courtrooms for centuries outside the spotlight of media attention.

Countless African Americans have seen this blind-eyed face of justice. They have had no one to stand up for them or anyone shinning a public spotlight on the mockery of justice that the system has presented in place of their right to trial by jury.

This leads me to two questions:
Is the jury system broken?

Does an 18th century concept in American jurisprudence, trial by jury, have any validity in 21st century America?

Surely, if Americans cannot divorce themselves of racial misconceptions and conditioning, which one could argue is apparently formed in vitro, a system designed to judge people who shared the same ethnicities in 1789 cannot survive the dichotomy of race and culture inherent in the new America created in 1865.

Jacksonville, Florida

February 22, 2014

ESSAY 10

How Do White Men Get Away With Killing Black Teenagers?

"Let the eagle scream! Again the burden of upholding the best traditions of Anglo-Saxon civilization has fallen on the sturdy shoulders of the American Republic. Once more a howling mob of the best citizens in a foremost state of the Union has vindicated the self-evident superiority of the white race. The case was perfectly clear; it was not that murder had been done, for us Americans are not squeamish at mere murder. Off and on we do more of that kind of thing than most folk. Moreover, there was not much of a murder-only the crazed act of a drunken man quite unpremeditated. The point is he was black."

W. E. B. DuBois
"Triumph," The Crisis, September 1911

"Juror No. 8 (Creshuna Miles) shows how a misinformed juror can throw a trial," said Teemo Luciano, his frustration spilling over after watching Miles appear on CNN to recount her thoughts on jury deliberations in the Michael Dunn murder trial.

Luciano, who works in the entertainment industry in Los Angeles, offered his comments after the conclusion of the second of two high-profile murder trials in Florida.

The trials involved the killings of two black teenagers by white men. Each ended without either man facing any consequences for killing the teenagers.

Miles, a 19 year-old African American woman, was one of two African American women on the jury. In spite of the fact their presence on the jury was secured by the Civil Rights Act of 1875, Miles does not think race played a part in the jury deliberations.

Since the beginning, jury service for any white American, born or naturalized, has come with the privilege of skin color.

The prosecutorial teams charged with bringing Zimmerman and Dunn to justice fell on the shoulders of Florida State Attorney, Angela B. Corey.

She is the granddaughter of Syrian immigrants and is a registered Republican. In the Zimmerman trial, she was appointed as special prosecutor in the case by Gov. Rick Scott (R-Fla.).

She received her assignment in the Dunn case by virtue of her job as state attorney for Duval County. A job she was elected to by the people in Florida's fourth judicial circuit, the site of the Jordan Davis murder.

In both cases, Corey's prosecutorial team has come under fire for a number of perceived trial tactical errors. For purposes of this essay we will address the jury selection process by the demographics.

As of the 2010 census, 51 percent of the voters in Duval County were registered as Republicans and 47 per cent were registered as Democrats. Sixty-one percent of the Duval County population is white and 30 percent is African American.

In Seminole County, Fla., the site of the Zimmerman trial, 81.4 percent of the population is white and only 11.8 percent is African American.

Why is this important?

Jury lists are culled from the voter registration rolls. Moreover, the greater percentage of a group's representation in the population, the greater the odds that a majority of that group's members will comprise the jury veneer and ultimately the empanelled jury that will decide the outcome of the trial.

In the Trayvon Martin case, Zimmerman got off "scot-free," an English word derived from the Scandinavian word "Skat." It was first used in the 16th century to denote one who had avoided justice. There were no African Americans on the Zimmerman jury.

Although Dunn did not get off scot-free, he was able to avoid, for the foreseeable future, a murder conviction for killing Jordan Davis. There were two African Americans on the Dunn jury.

While the law does not require any specific percentage of ethnic representation on juries, it can be argued that this ethnic group was underrepresented on the jury. Because African Americans make up 30 percent of the population in Duval County there should have been 3.6 (or, by rounding off, four) African Americans on this jury.

Whites were overrepresented on this jury because they make up 61 percent of the population. Therefore they should have only had 7.32 (or, by rounding off, seven) whites on this jury. There were eight whites on the jury instead.

Now that we have the demographics out of the way, the big problem the prosecution has in the selection of these two juries is the fact that prosecutors are routinely accustomed to prosecuting black defendants, oftentimes for having committed crimes against whites and occasionally for black-on-black crime.

Because prosecutors chiefly prosecute black defendants, they tend to work hard to exclude black jurors. They have very little experience in counting upon black jurors to be a factor in the jury room.

Before the Supreme Court stepped in and stopped the practice in Batson v. Kentucky, prosecutors without blinking an eye would exclude every black person on the jury veneer.

By representing the interests of Martin and Davis, Corey was asked to do something she and the jury system were not accustomed to doing: Seek justice for African Americans who were victims of white rage and violence.

A case in point, last year Corey defeated a "stand your ground" claim in prosecuting Marissa Alexander, an African American women who fired a warning shot over the head of her husband after he threatened to kill her.

Corey had no problems getting a jury to reject Alexander's self-defense claim. Alexander received a 20-year sentence.

This leads us to voir dire, the jury selection process, the most important aspect in the trial. Simply put, it appears, Corey and her team did not have ample experience in selecting African American jurors.

Moreover, in neither case was there any courtroom participation of an African American assistant state attorney. Such participation would have been very beneficial in assisting the state in developing a jury profile for African American members found in the jury veneer.

Without this kind of assistance the prosecutorial team of Corey, Guy, et al. were left with two millennials, born in this century, and too young to have a personal segregation history and far less educated on the history of the enslavement of African people to make an educated judgment on the motivations of Dunn in engaging the teenagers in an argument over loud music.

What this jury needed, from the state's perspective, were several African Americans who could decipher the nuances inherent in a middle-aged white man's order to a carload of black teenagers demanding they turn their music down.

Jacksonville, Florida
February 24, 2014

ESSAY 11

Speaking truth in the jury room

"People who treat other people as less than human must not be surprised when the bread they have cast on the waters comes floating back to them, poisoned."

James Baldwin,
"No Name in the Street"

Voir dire is French for "speak the truth." It is the process of questioning prospective jurors in search of a jury that is not biased toward one side in a trial.

The goal is to select a venire or panel that will speak the truth after reviewing all of the knowable facts. A jury must determine which set of facts speaks the truth.

In the Zimmerman and Dunn trials, it appears to me that both juries focused their attention on the law of the case. This is in direct violation of one of the jury instructions given to them by the trial judges.

When I was a trial lawyer, there were two things I wanted the prospective jurors to understand, which I think the prosecution failed to do in the Zimmerman and Dunn trials. Those two things involve the role of the Judge in a criminal trial and the role of the jury in a criminal trial.

I believe that both of these breaches contributed to the public perception that the jury system is dysfunctional when it comes to justice for African-Americans involved as victims or defendants in the system:

There are two judges in the courtroom during the trial. The presiding judge is the judge of the law. The other judge in the courtroom is the jury. The jury is the judge of the facts.

Back when I was a criminal litigator, whatever dichotomies were present in my case, I wanted to explore them with the jury to ensure that when they spoke the truth of what happened, their verdict was not tainted due to a bias or prejudice toward my side of the dichotomy. Dichotomies can be racial, sexual, educational, etcetera.

Based upon the questions of the Zimmerman and Dunn juries, the jurors were focused on understanding the legal principles of "defense of self" and "stand your ground."

This was not their job. The law as written is immutable. There was no need for these juries to analyze the law. Their job was to determine which set of facts was true, period.

For instance, in the Zimmerman case, did Zimmerman pick on Trayvon Martin or did Martin jump Zimmerman because he was a thug out for no good?

The Zimmerman jury had multiple opportunities based upon the totality of the evidence to discredit Zimmerman's changing version of what had transpired.

They also had a jury instruction that told them they could find that Zimmerman was not telling the truth and could disregard his entire testimony via police statements. This jury, however, concluded that Zimmerman's account of events were in fact how this tragedy unfolded.

The same is true in the Dunn case. The factual question for the jury was: Given the totality of the evidence, did Dunn shoot an unarmed man?

His flight from the scene alone was ample evidence to find that he had not testified truthfully regarding seeing a gun in Jordan Davis' hand.

Both juries deflected the shortcomings of their job as judge of the facts and pointed their fingers at Florida's "stand your ground" statute.

These two juries got out of hand because the prosecution failed to explore the dichotomy of race during voir dire.

The defense attorney boasted during a pre-verdict press conference that he did not mention anything about race.

It was not to his advantage to empower the two African-American women on the jury to identify with the four young African-American men in the bullet-riddled Sports Utility Vehicle.

On the other hand, the state in both cases needed to ferret out any bias that prospective jurors might tend to lend toward the white men left standing in both altercations. Failure to do so was a dereliction of duty.

The way I handled the delicate job of finding racially biased jurors and to educate whites on the venire to the complexities of race in the case was to tell a story about my collegiate baseball playing days.

At the end of the story, I was the racist, who after sliding into home plate, had dumped the opposing catcher to the turf because he was the only white player on the field and the only white person in the ballpark. Racism, after all, has to do with power, the type of power that renders ones adversary powerless to object to capricious treatment.

This story caused white jurors to relax. They did not expect the racist in the story to be the black lawyer standing before them. Also, white jurors understood the supreme advantage in holding majority status. They could feel the helplessness of the white catcher all alone on James Washington Field in Tuskegee Institute, Alabama.

I used this story to illustrate how good people sometimes in the heat of the moment do and say things they later regret.

In 2000, I defended a black man accused of malice murder along with three other black men in the death of a popular 17-year-old white high school wrestler.

We started voir dire on the first Monday morning following the turn of the century. We had about 1,200 jurors to interview. They were all seated in the courtroom as we questioned them in groups of 12.

I told this story 100 times. Every member on the panel heard it each time. During breaks, court personnel would approach and ask me, if I was safe or out. They were hanging onto every word of this story, each time I told it to a fresh group of twelve.

On Wednesday of that week, at the end of the day the judge asked everyone to leave the courtroom, except the lawyers.

He advised me that a deputy came to him that morning and told him about a disparaging remark a juror had made about me on Monday morning as he was coming into the courthouse.

The juror asked the deputy, "What do you think about that nigger lawyer from Atlanta."

The juror was struck for cause, but more importantly, that told me we had resonated with the jurors over the racial issue.

The comment was as disparaging on Monday as it was on Wednesday, but the deputy did not come forward until he had heard my story over and over again for two and solid days. The deputy had to decide if he was being racist in not disclosing this fact to the court. When he came forward, I had a good idea what the outcome of the trial would be. Two weeks later my client was acquitted of malice murder.

Race is a pervasive issue in our society, and it cannot be overlooked in criminal cases involving members of different racial and ethnic groups.

The lawyer who does not talk about race during jury selection is doomed to have a jury that may have a bias that could have been discovered if the appropriate questions had been asked up front.

Jacksonville, Florida
February 28, 2014

ESSAY 12

On the Evil in the Abyss

"*Every human being that believes in capital punishment loves killing, and the only reason they believe in capital punishment is because they get a kick out of it. Nobody kills anyone for love, unless they get over it temporarily or otherwise.*"

Clarence Darrow, Public Debate, and Resolved: That Capital Punishment is a Wise Public Policy
September 23, 1924

"Why are you going down there," my editor of thirty-three and a half years queried with a bit of concern and pride in her voice.

It was a fair question. Down there was the abyss, the Jackson Diagnostic and Classification Prison, which temporarily houses every person penalized in the Georgia criminal industrial complex, as well as Georgia's infamous "death row."

Many of you know that in another life I was a criminal defense lawyer of some note in the state of Georgia.

During that period of my career I handled five death penalty cases. I ended my legal career without losing a man to the Georgia electric chair, which was called "Old Smokey" by prison officials. Since I left the practice, Georgia now puts it condemned citizens to death by lethally injecting a cocktail of deadly drugs into the convict's veins that stops the heart from beating.

In addition to losing a close personal friend (many times the only friend the criminally accused has is the guy trying to save his life), I dreaded the thought of sitting through the legal murder of my client.

I worked hard not to ever be placed in that position. As history records, I never was. I saved all five souls from state execution.

So, why go now? Why go to oppose the execution of a man found guilty by a jury of his peers? Why?

It is a hard question to answer. Something tugged at the core of my being the morning of the planned execution, so I went. I had visited the abyss on one other occasion, to see a member of "Death Row" who wanted to reopen his case.

The late Johnnie Cochran had told this young man and a group of foreign benefactors that I was the best lawyer to handle his appeal. I did not have any experience in the post-conviction phase of death penalty work as I had never had a case that went that far.

Yet out of respect to Johnnie Cochran, I drove down to the abyss and met with this young man. I will keep his name anonymous for fear any publicity may speed up the day he is required to be put to sleep by medication administered at the behest of the State of Georgia.

I had arranged to stop by one day on my return trip to Atlanta from a court appearance in Bibb County. My hearing in Bibb County lasted longer than expected and I arrived at the gate ten minutes late and learned that you can't be late by one minute or you lose your privilege to see your client.

So I scheduled a return trip. When I stepped inside the prison and was ushered to the "Death Row" wing, I had an eerie feeling as the steel door shut behind me. It banged and it clanked.

I had been in sundry jails throughout Georgia, Alabama and Florida, but the sounds they produced were not as profound in describing the utter helplessness one must feel trapped behind these doors knowing that the only escape is death at the hands of the government.

"What if I was trapped in here and could not get out," I thought?

We turned down a dimly lighted hallway with rows of barred cells on either side. Men came to the bars, some smiled, others spoke greetings; yet others nodded, acknowledging my presence.

My client had been bragging that Johnnie Cochran was sending a lawyer to see him. We came to an open area without a door. The room had two chairs. The corrections officer offered me a seat and said my client would be brought up soon.

Shortly, he appeared. We embraced. He told me his story. It was, as you can imagine, a tragic story of being in the wrong place, at the wrong time, and with all the wrong people. He was convicted of murder under the "party to the crime" theory. Under this theory anyone who conspired to commit a felony that results in the death of another human being is as guilty as the person who committed the actual murder.

Ironically, all other participants in this brutal murder beat the rap or were given prison sentences which were completed many years ago; including the person who bludgeoned the young victim to death. Fancy this, justice in America.

He already had a fine post-conviction lawyer and I declined to participate in the case. The doors of the prison banged and clanked shut behind me.

Although breathing fresh air and feeling the sun on my face that afternoon, I could not tell if I was free or trapped inside of a judicial vortex that could not give a hoot about truth apart from the legal fiction that emerges as the rule of law.

"So why go now," the question persists?

There is something compelling about a man being put to death where there is so much doubt. When explaining reasonable doubt to a jury I would often say:

"If the evidence makes the inside of your brain go 'aw', or 'wait a minute', then that's reasonable doubt." There is something about the recantation evidence by several eye witnesses that made my mind go, "aw, wait a minute."

So I went.

I boarded a bus sponsored by Al Sharpton's National Action Network (NAN). The group was mostly Christian, it included some Muslims, and a Christian prayer was prayed, led by the remarkable Rev. Vizion Jones. We had a pleasant ride down to Jackson, Georgia.

We were met by State Troopers in riot gear and several police dogs. The storm troopers herded us into a corral as if we were cattle, hogs, horses or perhaps slaves.

They then circled the perimeter in full battle gear and informed those who came as part of a prayer vigil, they were not allowed to leave the corral. Some of the older members grew faint and needed a comfort break. They walked out and had to plead with the authorities to be let back inside the corral.

As the day wore on and tension mounted over the pending state murder of Troy Davis, two storm troopers came to the entrance of the corral and blocked the passage way out.

We were placed in this human zoo with two picnic tables to accommodate at least 100 men, women and children. Many of the adults were in their senior years.

The sun beat down upon us as there were neither trees nor awnings to shade us from its rays.

Meanwhile, the international, national, and local media would spend some time watching the humans in the zoo and then would run for the shade of the tents that had been provided to accommodate them. We had come as a prayer vigil, to support the family of Troy Davis. The three other times that Troy Davis had faced the grim reaper the prayer vigil had come in peace.

Yet the State of Georgia felt compelled to turn the abyss into an armed camp. They stared at us as speaker after speaker told the storm troopers that "we are not afraid of you, because we have come in the name of the Lord." Some spirits were convicted, some hearts were hardened. Nevertheless, we prayed.

When the 7:00 o'clock hour drew nigh (the designated time for the execution), without a word from the Supreme Court staying the execution, grown men; albeit warriors, broke down and cried like babies. Women fell to their knees, some prostrate and wept. I walked the circle consoling those who mourned. Then word came that Troy still lived, his execution had been halted minutes before the lethal drip was to start flowing into his veins. I fell to my knees and wept.

Now there was the waiting game as Supreme Court Justice Clarence Thomas had agreed to present Davis' motion to the full court for consideration. Those with a legal education knew it now came down to whether Justice Kennedy, who is usually the swing vote in these tight cases, could be persuaded to halt the execution. The laity wondered if Justice Clarence Thomas would for once in his life make a ruling that helped his people.

Sometime around 9:00 pm, I got this eerie feeling; the same feeling that I would get when the jury had reached a verdict in my cases. If I saw more deputies in the courtroom than had been there all week during the trial, I knew the verdict did not favor my client.

Around 9:45 pm a rumor began circulating that a decision had been reached and as soon as Justice Thomas could write the order it would be delivered to the abyss.

Coinciding with this rumor was the sudden appearance of an excessive number of state police cruisers into the area along Prison Boulevard with sirens blasting and lights swirling.

Then more storm troopers surrounded the prayer vigil compound. This told me Clarence Thomas had passed up yet another opportunity to "man up" to race and culture in America.

I began to prepare my friends. When the

word came via Ben Jealous, President of the National Association for the Advancement of Colored People (NAACP) that the execution had begun we thanked God for entertaining our petition.

As the life force passed from Troy Davis' body into eternity, a refreshing air of affirmation came upon the pray vigil and every man, woman and child knew what had to be done. We had to get up in the morning and begin the fight to ensure this never happened again.

Jackson, Georgia

September 22, 2011

Closing Argument

"We hold these truths to be self-evident that all men [people] are created equal and endowed by their creator with certain inalienable rights to life, liberty and the pursuit of happiness."

Declaration of Independence

July 4, 1776

Twelve little essays symbolic of twelve peers who are called upon to speak the truth of what happened in events they were not privy to attend. The best way for the American jury system to work is for good people to show up for jury duty when summed, focused on rendering justice beyond the pale of the legal fictions they will be presented with in court.

The jury system as envisioned by the framers of the Constitution depends upon good fair-minded people willing to lay aside their business interests for however long it takes to get to the truth of legal disputes between their neighbors.

Therefore, the major reform needed in the jury system is a reformation in the mind of the public towards jury duty. It is a sacred trust for those who would be free. It is a trust that must of necessity be exercised with care and diligence to the truth.

Dear reader, justice in the court begins with your willingness to show up for jury duty without your mind focused on finding an excuse to be stricken from jury service. Some poor soul is languishing in a system of injustice hoping that someone will hear the justice of his or \her cause and render a fair verdict that speaks to the truth of their involvement in the issue at bar.

Truth knows no skin color. It does not favor the privileged, or the strong, or the wealthy. It does not despise the poor, or the blacks, or the immigrants, or the children, or the women, or the gay, or the straight, or the mentally ill. Truth is stripped bare of biases and prejudices. It knows only that which is true; as well as, Semper Novi quid ex Injustice, which is to say truth always knows injustice.

On July 27, 2014, I previously shipped this manuscript to the publisher. I thought the problems of the jury system could easily be fixed as stated above. At that time, I believed the problems, although systemic, could be easily handled by good people showing up for jury duty willing to get to the bottom of the controversies that interrupted their personal lives and brought them to the courthouse.

My postulation was validated on October 1, 2014, when a Duval County, Florida jury brought back a guilty verdict on the charge of first-degree murder against Michael Dunn in the shooting death of a black teenager, because the teenager refused to turn his music down to a level acceptable to Dunn.

It was the second time Dunn faced a jury in the death of Jordan Davis. The first case had ended in a mistrial in 2013, which caused many, including this writer, to question the fairness of jury trials where the issues were racially charged.

After Dunn was convicted following his second trial, Ron Davis, Jordan's father, seemed to agree with my hypothesis. In front of the courthouse, he told reporters moments after the jury verdict was published in open court, that the verdict was "a shining example that you could have a jury made of mostly white people, white men, that delivers justice in a racially-charged case."

Davis was as optimistic as I was over the long-term impact of the jury verdict. "Hopefully, this is a start where we don't have to look at the makeup of a jury anymore," Davis said.

The second Dunn trial was held with far less media attention than the first trial. Other than the Jacksonville, Florida, community where the trial was held, hardly anyone in America knew that the trial was in process. This was a far cry from the media circus that engulfed the first trial.

Justice had come full circle and allowed the truth to speak. It spoke volumes. The decibels of truth overtook the loud noise ringing in Dunn's ear that Thanksgiving season when he riddled Davis' body with bullets.

Finally, justice had appeared in the round. It had come full circle. At any rate, I thought it had appeared just as I had envisioned it would when I set out to publish this collection of essays.

However, I honestly did not expect justice to show up as quickly as it did; certainly not without *Justice in the Round*, as a public guide.

Little did we know at the time, there were forces at play that would lead to a monumental distrust in the legal system and all that we thought we had gained from the Dunn conviction would come to naught.

On July 17, 2014, Eric Garner, a 43 year-old a black man married with children was choked to death by Daniel Pantaleo, a white police officer in Staten Island, New York, after the officer accused Garner of selling illegal cigarettes. Garner, much bigger than any of the police officers on the scene was wrestled to the ground by way of a choke hold, a procedure outlawed by the New York Police Department because it had led to deaths in the past. He complained to the arresting officers that he could not breathe. He lay on the sidewalk, in the hot sun, and died.

There were rumblings in the streets. Protests sprang up. Rev. Al Sharpton was in his element. He had a protest on his home turf to conduct. He called out New York Mayor Bill de Blasio who has a half-black son, who looks more black than white. "It could have been your son," Sharpton posited.

De Blasio, married to a black woman who has given him a son and daughter, promised a thorough investigation. Following the release of the medical examiner's report which listed the cause of death as a homicide, a grand jury was impaneled to look into Garner's death.

Meanwhile, in the heartland, on August 9, 2014, Michael Brown, a black teenager, walked from a store is stopped by Darren Wilson, a white police officer. An altercation ensued, and Brown, who is much larger than the Ferguson Missouri officer, is shot multiple times.

Instantly, he dies in the street.

He lay on the street for four and one-half hours while the police conduct their investigation.

With each minute that passed while Brown's lifeless body laid in the street, the crowd grew and became angrier and angrier.

Eye witness accounts spread that Brown was shot after holding his arms in the air in the sign of surrender. Suddenly, the crime scene turns into a combat zone as the police hustle in military equipment, which many in the crowd had only seen on television news reports from Afghanistan or Iraq.

Tensions flared.

The town rioted and demonstrated. Sharpton came to town. He asked the protestors to pay membership dues to his organization, the National Action Network, and the protesters, many of whom were listed as statistics in the double-digit unemployment suffered by blacks in Ferguson, told him he was not welcome. They would lead their own protest fueled on sheer passion and energy and without money. He scurried back to New York to manage the Garner demonstration.

The protests became ugly. Ferguson's black community looked like Palestine on the West Bank with protesters hurling rocks at the police and tear gas canisters shot into the crowd by those sworn to protect and serve peaceful public dissent.

President Barack Obama asked the people of Ferguson to be calm. He dispatched his Attorney General, Eric Holder, to Missouri. On the state level, a grand jury was convened to look into the shooting death of Brown. Holder asked the U. S. Attorney's office in Missouri to open a case to determine whether Brown's civil rights had been violated.

Very little is known about the workings of a grand jury. By law, their work is done in secret. While anyone whose name appears on the voting rolls is subject to be called to serve on a petit jury, a French term meaning small, which is the name given to a trial jury because only twelve members serve on a petit jury at one time, as opposed to a grand jury, which can consist of twelve to twenty-three members.

I have been on the voter's rolls since Nixon was president. On numerous occasions, I have been summoned to appear for petit jury duty, but not once have I been summoned to serve on a grand jury. I know of only two people from my community who have ever served on a grand jury. Although many are eligible by law, only a few are called to serve.

Why is this? I am not entirely sure.

The grand jury system stems from old common law as practiced in Great Britain before the enactment of the American written legal code and judicial decisions. Many countries that used this method to investigate whether or not to bring charges against a citizen of their country have eliminated the use of the grand jury system. However, these methods still persist in the United States of America.

Under the old common law, a private citizen could bring a complaint against their neighbor by taking the complaint to a grand jury that would determine if what was alleged constituted a crime. If the grand jury determined a crime had been committed, it would authorize the complaining private citizen to prosecute the case. Obviously, this prosecutorial system was fraught with abuse, so the sheriff assumed the prosecutorial duties once the grand jury had determined that it was likely a crime had been committed. Eventually, this system evolved into a designated prosecutor, which is the system in place in all 50 states.

Under the common law system, it was thought that a grand jury panel would be helpful in weeding out frivolous complaints by neighbors who had a personal axe to grind with each other. The grand jury was utilized in the colonies before the revolution.

The framers of The Constitution of the United States of America felt so strongly about the presentments of a grand jury that they codified this practice in the Fifth Amendment to the Constitution. The same amendment that gave us due process rights, protected us from being tried for the same crime twice, and required the state to compensate us when it takes our property for a public use, begins by authorizing grand juries to look into possible criminal conduct.

"No person shall be held to answer for a capital, or otherwise infamous crime, unless on a presentment or indictment of a grand jury..."[36]

In some states, the district attorney can bring a case without going to a grand jury. The prosecutors in both Ferguson and New York punted this responsibility to the grand jury. Each could have made a decision to indict the officers

---

[36] The Constitution of the United States of America, Amendment V

involved, thus ensuring that the evidence would have a full and public hearing.

Most states allow police officers to testify before a grand jury when charges are being contemplated against them. Both the state of Missouri and New York allow this practice. In these cases, the police officers involved testified before the grand juries. So there was nothing unusual in allowing officers to take advantage of their opportunity to speak directly to their respective grand juries.

The problem lies in how both cases were presented to the grand juries by the prosecutors in Ferguson and New York. The public record indicates that both prosecutors presented far more evidence than was necessary to "indict a ham sandwich."

Obviously, it does not take much evidence to prosecute a poor ham sandwich, and this has become the standard that most prosecutors apply when presenting cases to grand juries. Grand jury discussions usually leave out the full details for the trial jury to sort out after a full airing of all of the evidence deemed necessary to gain a conviction.

According to records released from the Ferguson grand jury (we can only speculate that the same applies to the New York grand jury), the prosecution went beyond asking the various witnesses what they saw or heard. The prosecutor actually cross-examined them, punching perceived holes in their eye witness account of what happened on those fateful days.

One member of the Ferguson grand jury has filed a lawsuit seeking the right to break the lifetime ban on discussing how events unfolded during the grand jury meetings, as grand jury members are sworn to secrecy once a case has been presented to them.

According to court documents, the unnamed grand juror alleges that the prosecution treated the Brown case differently than it did the other cases that had been presented during the term of this particular grand jury and that the conclusion reached did not reflect this grand juror's impression of the evidence that had been presented.

This juror's challenge underscores the uneasiness felt in black America when it was announced the Ferguson grand jury failed to indict Wilson for the death of Brown.

If the majority of black Americans were "simmering over Zimmerman," as this writer posited back in 2013 when the petit jury verdict came back in favor of George Zimmerman, the Ferguson and New York grand juries, under their accustomed cloud of secrecy, caused blacks throughout the country to sizzle.

Where is the justice? Has the African American ingredient in the melting pot caused the pot to boil over into the streets of America?

This question summed up the bewilderment felt in black America over these two grand jury decisions. Hopes dashed, faith in the system wavering and anger boiling beneath the surface. The collective spirit of African Americans seemed to paraphrase Medgar Evers quoted elsewhere in these essays: it seemed as if the scales of justice would never come into balance and would always tilt towards the lighter shades of grey in the American populous.

It is one thing for a person to undergo a trial by jury, where the evidence is laid bare before the eye of public scrutiny, and come out of that process exonerated, but quite another proposition to have the facts weighed behind closed doors, votes taken, proceedings sealed and then an announcement that no further action will be taken on this matter.

Stultifying in the unspoken nuances of language, the seal of approval of the Ferguson and New York prosecutorial system left black Americans and others numbed to the point of speechlessness. The people in those communities, joined by others from around the country, took to the streets to protest a seeming lack of care for the lives of black teenagers.

Suddenly, several decades of referring to Americans who trace their linage to enslaved Africans as African Americans reverted back to the vernacular of the 1960s and blacks became the term of choice of news writers.

Perhaps, only by looking through a black and white prism can the significance of the problem be fully understood. To refer to the demonstrators as black points out the fact that dark-skinned Africans have never been accepted as Americans like Europeans who immigrated to these shores. Their black skin will always highlight the sins of western civilization sandwiched between the Atlantic and Pacific Oceans. As the Charlie Hebdo assassination reveals, even when Africans without American citizenship commit a bad act in faraway places, well-respected journalists like CNN's Chris Cuomo, will identify them as African Americans.[37]

In Ferguson and New York, young African Americans without a segregated past took to the streets in protest of legal decisions which seemed to proclaim that "black lives do not matter." They were joined by other young Americans, also without a segregated past, who traced their linage back to Europe.

This confluence of history joins black and white heirs of the 20th century "Reconstruction" that was brought forth by way of legislation and judicial decisions instigated by the civil rights movement in voting, housing, education, employment, and public accommodations.

All of the above have been enjoyed by black and white millennials without the added burden of struggling to gain access to the American dream by black children. Or the burden of restricting access to them by white children. This cannot be said of any other generation in American history.

When I was thirteen years old and one of a hand-full of black students in the newly integrated local junior high school, I seldom, if ever, got praise from whites, neither from the teacher nor the kids my age. Thirty years later a white

---

[37] http://www.mediaite.com/tv/anderson-cooper-corrects-cuomos-description-of-french-terrorist-as-african-american/

classmate from those early days of integration and I had children in the same private high school in Atlanta.

He confided in me that he had wanted to come to my aid, especially when one overly aggressive, racist teacher was on a tear to run me back to the black school, but he dared not speak up for fear of being ostracized as a "Nigger Lover." That's a label that could have been a "kiss of death" to an upstanding white boy in the 1960s before he had a chance to prove his worth among other white kids.

Thus this confluence of history brings together a generation of Americans who care a lot less about the color of their friend's skin than their parents, or their grandparents, or their great-grandparents before them. What would have been a precipice fraught with danger in the past now holds the genesis for eventual success.

As my extended family and support system met to celebrate Kujichagulia at Kwanzaa 2014, the millennial members of the clan chose the topic of Ferguson and Staten Island: Do the street protests have relevancy and can they be sustained, they posited?

There was worry and concern over this issue etched in the faces of the millennials. If my generation was concerned, and surely the majority of us are, it did not show on our faces as it did on the faces of our millennial off-spring. I came away from this gathering with the realization that this issue really matters to millennials. They are frightened for their future survival in America.

First, Ben, a millennial who was born in Kenya, offered that Dr. Ron Karenga, the father of Kwanzaa, had missed the mark in defining the term Kujichagulia. Karenga had, in the mid 1960s, defined it as a way: "To define ourselves, name ourselves, create for ourselves and speak for ourselves," in short, "self-determination."

According to Ben, Kujichagulia in Swahili, his native tongue, means "to make right choices." He concedes that Karenga got the other six principles correct.

It was important for the young people at this gathering to know they were making correct choices in being in the streets. They asked me to be the first to opine on the relevancy and sustainability of the "Black Lives Matter" protests.

A short while into my presentation, the generational divide was evident when I proclaimed these demonstrations as a young people's movement for human rights led by young people who do not need Rev. Al Sharpton and other civil rights leaders to spearhead their protest. This is not a knock on Sharpton or any other leaders who cut their teeth in the movement for civil rights; it is an acknowledgement that the paradigm has shifted, which must of necessity have a new generation of leaders to play the game.

Two years ago, I secured a small role in *The Final Punch*, a movie about the last fight that Muhammad Ali fought in The Bahamas, on December 1, 1981, against Trevor Berbick. The movie is set to be released in 2015.

Many people do not recall this fight because by the time Ali had secured a permit to fight he had long since overstayed his time in the ring. Perhaps his last fight where he had full command of his boxing arsenal was the *"Thrilla in Manila,"* against Joe Frazier on October 1, 1975. However, Ali stayed in the ring six more years, leaving as a punch-drunk, journeyman fighter, reminiscent of the Archie Moore, who Ali had beaten into retirement by a Technical Knockout in four rounds, during his youth. Leaders like Ali have a hard time discerning when it is time to get off center stage.

The young people agreed with this assessment. Several "baby boomers" from my generation quickly objected. They interrupted my speech with the battle cries of the Civil Rights movement. One Dashiki wearing brother from Buffalo waxed eloquently, as Dashiki wearing brothers did in the 1960s, stringing $100 words together in sentences to desultorily proclaim nothing of substance that could give direction to the young people laying their lives on the line in streets across America in the name of "Black Lives Matter."

The cause of this generational chasm is due to the successes of their Civil Rights movement elders. Many baby boomers, this writer included, left the safe haven of their college campuses and raised the conscience of America from the streets. Our goal, and the goal of the elder statesmen of our day, was the elimination of the vestiges of second-class citizenship. Baby Boomers won that battle.

In the past thirty years they have been waging a war to protect the spoils gained in war with their country over full citizenship rights, while, at the same time, attempting to illicit the support of their progenies in the war to preserve civil rights won on the Edmund Pettis Bridge in Selma, in Kelly Ingram Park in Birmingham, in the Burroughs of New York, and on rural dusty roads across America.

The kids were slow to warm to hardships that do not exist in their lifetime. This all began to change with the message that came out of Sanford, Jacksonville, Detroit, Ferguson, and Staten Island. The message was loud and clear: Jim Crow laws may have been defeated, but the social mores that undergirded those laws were alive and well.

In short, it is no longer a question of attending any school you dream of attending, the question for this generation becomes their very survival. Thus the slogan, "Black Lives Matter" was introduced into the national lexicon by three creative women, community organizers Alicia Garza, Patrisse Cullors, and Opal Tometi, following Zimmerman's acquittal for the killing of Trayvon Martin. This phrase took on a life of its own after the "No Bills of Indictment" were handed down in quick succession in Ferguson and New York.

While the energy of my generation was spent in gaining access to the institutions and to the benefits of American life, for young people today, "The fundamental question is how do we create a world where black lives matter," according to Garza.[38]

The paradigm has shifted to the human rights of the individual to live out their lives without being short-changed by a projectile from the barrel of a gun in the hands of a police officer. Baby Boomers have not gotten that yet, but we all will come to the realization that we fought and won our battle so that the present age could wage war on the ultimate front for human dignity.

This is what our ancestors asked the landed gentry to do coming out of the period of enslavement: Get over the fact that you no longer have free labor to do whatever comes to your mind, whenever it comes to mind, and accept those you formally enslaved with the human dignity offered to any other American.

The goal, therefore, for this generation of patriots is to secure their survival, thereby securing their place in American life and development. This is an achievable goal. The alternative is unfathomable. America cannot live out her creed of justice for all if young people, black, brown, yellow and white, do not take the reins of this movement and propel the struggle to its next logical conclusion.

There is a historical record that suggests the millennials are justified in creating a climate in 21st century America where black lives matter. In 1971, Samuel F. Yette, a staff writer at Newsweek, published, *The Choice: the Issue of Black*

---

[38] "Meet the Bart-Stopping woman behind 'Black Lives Matter,'" Heather Smith, Grist, December 4, 2014

Survival in America, his seminal work which foretold the despair felt by young black people today.

"A people whom the society had always denied social value... had also lost economic value. Theirs was the problem of all black America: survival."[39]

"Black Americans," Yette argued in the 1970s, "are obsolete people."[40]

It has taken 40 years for Yette's postulation to gain such widespread acceptance among the very people he sought to warn in the last quarter of the 20th century. Thanks to Ferguson, Staten Island, and the vigilante killings of Trayvon Martin and Jordan Davis, the nation is awakening to the real possibility that "X" number of people can be eliminated from active participation on this planet.

Yette was not the only visionary to warn of the prospect that certain groups of people would become marginalized and targets for annihilation so that privileged groups could survive. In 1968, Dr. Paul R. Ehrlich, Professor of Biology and Director of Graduate Study for the Department of Biological Sciences, Stanford University, published his disturbing thesis, *The Population Bomb*, in which he argued that by the end of the 1970s, the population on the earth would exceed the earth's ability to produce enough food to feed the populous.

---

[39] The Choice: The Issue of Black Survival in America, Samuel F. Yette, Berkley Publishing Corp., 1975, pp. 14
[40] Ibid., pp. 14

Ehrlich theorized there are two ways to solve the imbalance of increased population and less food production. One is the control of the birth rate through the use of contraception devices, or by an increase in the death rate through "war, famine and pestilence,"[41] which Ehrlich noted "find us."[42] Today, we can add to Ehrlich's death list the Biblical "white horse" of infectious diseases that can lead to a pandemic in less affluent communities.

"Radical change is both necessary and inevitable because the present increases in human numbers and per capita consumption, by disrupting ecosystems and depleting resources, are undermining the very foundations of survival."[43]

If the summer of 2014 can be described as the summer that brought us the clear and present specter of black male deaths in the streets of America at the hands of certified police officers, then it will also be remembered as the summer of the Ebola scare which, although Ebola is caused by a virus that does not discriminate when it comes to the immune systems it will attack, nevertheless, the virus seems to disproportionately affect black people.

The future, Yette wrote, "[…] promised new martyrs, bigger jails, more wars (at home and abroad), data banks, wiretaps, and a genuinely

---

[41] The Population Bomb, Dr. Paul R. Ehrlich, Ballentine Books, New York, 1968, pp. 34
[42] Ibid., pp. 34
[43] Blue-Print for Survival, the Editors of The Ecologist, New American Library, 1972, pp. 3

regimented society, including the sharp curtailment of black college students, a white establishment take-over of black colleges, and psychological barbed wire around all learning institutions."[44]

There is no question that black millennials clearly understand they now have "skin in the game," and that by winning, they will have the opportunity to remake America into more than she has ever been rather than allowing her to regress into something less than the ideal promulgated to the world in the 18th century.

Pardon me Baby Boomers, but it is time to get out of the way and let young people engage in the third principle of the Kwanzaa Sabo, "Kujichagulia". That is to make the "right choices" for the survival of their generation, thereby defining America anew where justice knows only that which is just.

Media mogul Oprah Winfrey takes issue with the leadership approach of millennials. She, like most Baby Boomers, is operating from the perspective of the rules of engagement in a civil disobedience campaign for civil rights. This is, after all, how Boomers waged the war and gained concessions in American life.

Winfrey's criticism of the hash-tag "BlackLivesMatters" campaign as being leaderless, goal-less and without focus, gives national exposure to the Kwanzaa discussion held by my

---

[44] The Choice: The Issue of Black Survival in America, Samuel F. Yette, Berkley Publishing Corp., 1975, pp. 19

extended family at the close of 2014. She highlighted the riots and violence which occurred in Ferguson as something that did not exist during the civil rights movement.

However, she forgets the consternation Dr. King must have felt when Stokely Carmichael (Kwame Ture) urged marchers to become more militant in their protest. Not to mention the fact that Annie Lee Cooper, the character she plays in the critically-acclaimed movie, *Selma*, at the height of efforts to register to vote in Selma, Alabama, punched the notorious Sheriff Jim Clark in the face.

Moreover, it was a riot during an earlier march in Memphis, Tennessee, led by King which brought him back to Memphis on that fateful day he was assassinated. There have always been disruptions of peaceful demonstrations, even those led by Dr. King, the greatest architect of civil disobedience in America. So the riots in Ferguson are nothing new and should not be a black mark on the leadership style of the millennials at the helm of this movement.

Winfrey's criticism drew prompt resistance from one Montgomery, Alabama, native, J. Richardson, a Baby Boomer, who posited on social media: "Oprah better watch out, she is not immune from being boycotted."

Young people immediately took to cyberspace to checkmate Winfrey and to defend their movement. On January 2, 2015, @Big6domino tweeted: "What Oprah missed about hash-tag Ferguson is that each & every one of those protesters [is a] leader." @Big6domino closed with the hash-tag "ICantBreathe."

@Big6domino makes a good point. I was an early critic of the "Occupy Movement" because I did not understand its sense of parliamentary procedure or leadership style. I was in Troy Davis Park the evening Occupy Atlanta leaders refused to allow Congressman John Lewis to address their rally. I thought they did not have a clue how important Lewis was to their movement.

I was wrong.

Both the Occupy Movement and Black Lives Matter Movement are well-organized groups. They have a cadre of leaders who have learned the history of the FBI's plots against Dr. King, the Black Panther Party for Self-Defense, and other civil rights leaders during the tumultuous 1960s.

In order to protect their leadership, millennials do not project a single person as the leader of the group. Instead, current-day community organizers opt to disburse the power of leadership throughout the movement with the sure focus that the goal to achieve at the end of the day is that of human dignity.

This strategy works well for them. People show up, signs are created, slogans are shouted, and in every hamlet in the country, citizens are aware of the group's hue and cry for the human right to walk the streets of America without being profiled due to skin color, or age, or sexual orientation, which at the end of the day, could prevent a safe return to their abode.

In the struggle for human rights new leaders are being born overnight. They do not, for lack of a better term, have the same pedigree as leaders during the civil rights era, who oftentimes were hand-picked to represent the very best perceived attributes of African Americans.

Today's movement finds unlikely leadership from people who have taken upon themselves to simply do something. Like Aurille Lucier, a 20-year-old Atlanta spoken word artist, who defines her sexual orientation as "queer."

Lucier, troubled by the killing of Michael Brown, took to social media, the ecosystem of the 21st century; she asked for 10 people to come together in an act of solidarity for the protests that had sprung up in Missouri. From this single tweet, 5000 people showed up a week later and shut down travel on Interstate 20, Atlanta's downtown connector.[45]

The "Queer Activist," as she sometimes describes herself, was reluctant to take the helm of leadership because of the civil rights model for leadership.

"I was really worried that people would confuse me with Rosa Parks or confuse me with the picture that I had in my head of what movement leaders look like. And I didn't want to be confused with that because I didn't think I could be that."[46]

Crises have a way of revealing the essence of leadership. When the history of the human

---

[45] Aurielle Lucier: The (Free) Radical, By Rodney Carmichael, Creative Loafing, January 1-January 7, 2015, pp. 15
[46] Ibid pp. 15

rights movement is written it will have new heroes and heroines, as history will record the valiant deeds of Aurille Lucier, Alicia Garza, Patrisse Cullors, and Opal Tometi, as it has recorded the deeds of Fannie Lou Hammer, Rosa Parks, Amelia Boynton-Robinson, and Viola Liuzzo.

Following a surge in street demonstrations resulting from the grand jury decisions in Ferguson and New York, President Obama dispatched his Attorney General, Eric Holder, to major urban centers in the country in order to begin a dialogue on race and justice in America. One such visit brought Holder to Atlanta, Georgia, home for many leaders of the civil rights movement era, in early December 2014.

Lucier's activism earned her an invitation to tell Holder during his town hall meeting in Atlanta that the federal government must de-militarize state and local police departments.

Rev. Dr. C. T. Vivian, a Presidential Medal of Freedom recipient and Civil Rights icon, listened to all the speakers, including Holder and the demonstrators who verbally spared with Holder over the militarization of American streets and summed up the paradigm shift by speaking directly to the millennials: "This is your movement. How can I help you?"

Vivian grasps more fully than most of his contemporaries, that the battle for reparatory justice must be fought in the streets before the politicos can amass the muscle for transitional reparatory justice, albeit, a novation of old promises, to occur.

Meanwhile, the streets, mid-way into the second decade of this century, have become even more dangerous, perhaps more than any other time in American history. Suddenly, police officers are under siege throughout the country. As 2014 drew to a close, police officers, Wenjian Liu and Rafael Ramos, while sitting in their squad car parked on a street in New York, were executed by a lone gunman, who, in his mind, was apparently set on avenging the deaths of Michael Brown and Eric Garner.

Senseless is about the only word that describes the execution of Liu and Ramos, who, paradoxically, are non-white Americans that one can only imagine had their own unique stories of overcoming the challenges of American life.

As unfortunate as these assassinations were, the deaths point out the senselessness of the carnage on the streets of America today, and have forced the law enforcement community to come to grips with the grief and anguish felt by African American families in the crass deaths of young men like Martin, Davis, Brown, Garner, and other nameless victims of police and "stand your ground" violence.

Also, gang members have made internet postings challenging their cohorts in urban centers across America to ambush police officers as an answer to the growing incidents of young black men being killed by police on American streets. Attacks on police officers are at an all time high.

Gangs are the largest armed segment of the African American population. Albeit, many of these gang members are probably carrying guns without legal authority. I would venture to say, perhaps 99 percent of gun-toting gang members are under some type of court supervision that prohibits them from possessing a firearm.

Heretofore, gang activity has been relegated to turf battles with rival gangs. Their victims have largely been members of their own ethnic group, including far, far too many innocent bystanders. They are now turning their weapons on the police. This maneuver can only lead to further escalation of police violence and repression against ordinary American citizens.

The streets are likely to get more dangerous before peace is restored. The rhetoric is escalating as police officers and others are blaming President Obama and New York Mayor De Blasio for the officers' deaths in New York.

It is felt that somehow, by being sympathetic to victims of police violence, Obama and De Blasio have undermined the police in the discharge of their duties, making the streets less safe for them and making it more difficult for police officers to return home at the end of the day to the comfort of their loved ones.

As protesters prepare to take to the streets in 2015, they will be met with a police force on edge as officers attempt to carry out their mission to protect the protesters from counter protesters, and now, the clear and present danger of having to protect themselves from radicalized members of the public, both white separatist and black liberationist, who would do them harm.

Into the above mix, add armored tanks and other artillery of war (items usually found on the battlefields of Iraq and now in the arsenal of local police departments, compliments of the federal government's 1033 program) and the prospect of revolution in the streets just grew exponentially.

Staten Island clearly brings into focus Ronald Segal's prophecy in his 1966 book *The Race War*. In a chapter titled *The White World of the United States*, Segal opined, "What has long been happening in the South of the United States is now happening in the North - a development of racial stress to the degree where it threatens society itself with a nervous breakdown. And in both regions the clash is based upon fear and centered round [around] power."[47]

These are challenging times for American democracy as millennials have come to mistrust their government to administer the law justly, fairly and equitably without respect to skin color, national origin, religion, economic standing, gender or sexual preference. We are embarked upon a collision course between justice and anarchy in the streets.

Segal theorized in the year after passage of the 1965 Voting Rights Acts in the United States, that race war is inevitable. "In the rich world," he wrote, "of course they know how easily racial prejudice may be acquired, and what strenuous and subtle application is necessary then to remove it. The whites of English or American cities have to be gradually soothed and cajoled away

---

[47] The Race War, Ronald Segal, The Viking Press, Inc., 1966, pp. 181

from prejudice, their natural fears placated, and their frustrations relieved, lest impatience and compulsion incite their suspicions to fury."[48]

In short, to paraphrase my postulation in the third paragraph of this *closing argument*: There must be a reformation in the mind of the people towards others with whom they share this planet. We must come to realize that as law and order impacts the society as a whole by making us safe, injustice has a strong impact as well by making the society less safe for the enjoyment of "life, liberty and the pursuit of happiness."[49]

As Dr. King reminded us, "the arch of the moral universe is long, but it bends towards justice." It has in the past, and it will in these times of trouble. However, it will take women and men of courage to resist pandering either for "law and order" or for "down with the cops" rhetoric. If we as a society do not commit to establishing a color-blind system of justice in the courts, we will continue to experience disruptions in the streets, which could change the dynamics of America as we have known her to be.

Rushing headlong into the 21st century, America will either live out her creed of justice for all, as rooted in the written words of her 18th century founders, or there will be modern-day rebellions, and correspondingly, the streets will be devoid of peace and occupied by militias, survivalists, ethnic gangs, nationalized state guard units, and millennial patriots, each seeking

---

[48] Ibid., pp. 4
[49] The Declaration of Independence, 1776

their perspective of what law and order, freedom and justice, civil rights and human decency is in the streets of America.

And those Americans left lying in the streets will say, *Nomen iustitiam, iustitiam in circuitu.*

Which is to say, *my name is justice - justice in the round.*

The Cascades, Atlanta, Georgia
January 10, 2015

Also by Harold Michael Harvey

Paper Puzzle

Available at
www.paperpuzzle.net
www.haroldmichaelharvey.com
www.amazon.com

Follow Harold Michael Harvey on Social Media

Twitter: @hmichaelharvey

Facebook:
https://www.facebook.com/haroldmichael.harvey

Contact information

hmharvey@haroldmichaelharvey.com

Available for speaking engagements and book signings